How to
Play Poker
and Win

How to Play Poker and Win

BRIAN McNALLY

with   JOHN THOMPSON

BARRY McILROY

First published 2000 by Channel 4 Books

an imprint of Macmillan Publishers Ltd
Pan Macmillan, 20 New Wharf Road, London N1 9RR
Basingstoke and Oxford
Associated companies throughout the world
www.panmacmillan.com

ISBN 0 7522 7219 5

9

A CIP catalogue record for this book is available from the British Library.

Designed and typeset by Ben Cracknell Studios

Printed by Mackays of Chatham plc

This book accompanies the series *Late Night Poker* made for Channel 4 by Presentable Productions.

Producer: Rob Gardner

Contents

Introduction

**There are two times in a man's life when
he should not speculate, when he can't afford it,
and when he can.**
Mark Twain in *Pudd'n Head Wilson.*

The late Walter Matthau described poker as exemplifying 'all of the worst aspects of capitalism that have made our country so great'. Along with Hollywood road movies, the images of the 'rambling-gambling man'and the poker-playing cowboy, willing to risk all on the turn of a card, are abiding metaphors for the free-spirited American ideal. A recent Hollywood film, *Rounders* starring Matt Damon, realistically portrayed the game with all of its thrills and excitement. Set in New York's underground poker world, *Rounders* tells the story of a card player who attempts to leave behind the poker-playing rounds for a legitimate career and a chance for a new life with his girlfriend. However, the new life is short on the buzz of high-stakes poker games and the Damon character is soon drawn back to the poker table.

Rounders gives one perspective on the game of poker, but often poker games are played by groups of friends purely for enjoyment, with winning or losing being secondary to the social experience, and with the stakes often nothing more than matchsticks. Inventor Sir Clive Sinclair is perhaps the best known of all the players who have appeared on Channel 4's *Late Night Poker* series, and he plays socially in a private game. For him, poker is an opportunity to meet friends and pass an enjoyable evening. Sir Clive has played poker for about ten years and for a recreational player he has acquitted himself very well against the ranks of professionals in the series. I am not alone in believing that if he played as much as some of the rest of us, he would become a very formidable player indeed.

However, I would contend that to experience the true thrill of poker it should be played for stakes that matter to the players. If you are playing for a sum of money that is meaningful to you, your sense of excitement will be heightened, your palms will start to sweat, the adrenaline will start to pump in your bloodstream and you will experience a sense of risk rarely encountered in everyday life.

The purpose of this book is to introduce men and women, of all ages, to the thrills of playing poker. My task, and that of my co-authors, is primarily to help new players to get started, although the book also contains insights and tips so that more established players can improve their game. Most people, especially those who have watched *Late Night Poker*, will already have some idea about the basics of poker. However, it is only after long hours of play and some study that you will begin to appreciate the many skills needed to become a competent player. It takes longer still to appreciate all of the game's subtleties and to become a strong player.

It may be helpful at this stage to look briefly at the historical development of poker before explaining the rudiments of the modern game.

A Brief History of Poker

The origin of poker and the course of its early development is open to speculation. Some contend that it is a direct descendant of Poque, an old French game in which bluffing seems to have played a considerable part. It is possible that the name Poque derived from the French verb *pocher*, meaning to bluff. Others say that its origins go as far back as the ancient Persian game of As nas. An early Italian game called Il Frusso, played in the fifteenth century, also bears some similarity to poker. This game developed into Primiera in Italy, Primero in Spain and Le Mesle or Prime in France. It was introduced to England in the early seventeenth century where it later matured into a game named Post and Pair. As settlers from France, Spain, Italy and England emigrated to what eventually became the USA, they brought with them these various forms of what we can now call poker.

There is general agreement that the transformation of these early games into the modern form of 'draw poker' occurred in North America in the early part of the nineteenth century. The game was played by pioneers in the backwoods and gradually the word poker began to appear in writings and 'dime novels' of the period. The city of New Orleans is considered to be the place where poker first rose in popularity and developed a hold upon the American psyche. New Orleans citizens of French descent undoubtedly called it Poque, after the game played in France. In time, the game came to be played on the Mississippi River steamboats, where Poque was corrupted into the word 'poker', the name that remains today.

At the end of the nineteenth century, another poker variant developed, known as 'stud poker'. One version of this, five-card stud, became the card game of choice during the early to mid-twentieth century. This is the game that featured in the classic film *The Cincinnati Kid*.

The Modern Game

In the 1930s, a further variation, called 'seven-card stud', began to gain prominence and, along with draw poker, held sway until the late 1950s. Around this time, further alterations to the game took place, leading to the modern game of Texas Hold 'Em, which is played on *Late Night Poker*. Now, in the early twenty-first century, the three most popular poker variants are Texas Hold 'Em, Omaha and seven-card stud, all of which will be described in this book.

In recent years poker has turned into a television spectacle. For the past fifteen years an event called the World Series of Poker has been televised in the USA, while *Late Night Poker* has precipitated a considerable amount of interest in the game in the UK. British players have noticed a large influx of new players into poker since the start of the series and the majority of these newcomers say that the programmes awakened their interest in the game. One new departure of Channel 4's series is the use of under-table cameras, which allow the players' hands to be observed.

Throughout the book you will read about the guidelines that have helped my co-authors and myself to understand and win at poker. However, we don't make extravagant claims or pretend that the advice we give is either definitive or comprehensive. Learning poker can be compared to learning a new language (indeed, it has a patois all of its own) and it will take you many years to learn all of the game's intricacies. There is a complete new lexicon of words and phrases to be understood and a comprehensive glossary is included to help you master these terms.

There are several ways to learn how to play poker, with the 'hard knocks of experience' being perhaps the most expensive method. More positive ways include watching and listening critically to other players (particularly good ones, although you can also learn from weaker players' mistakes) as well as consulting books. Along with the TV series, this book will guide you towards a mastery of the game and will help you become a stronger player. Who knows, maybe you will feature on a future *Late Night Poker* series yourself!

Brian McNally

How to Play

**The urge to gamble is so universal
and its practice so pleasurable that
I assume it must be evil.**
Heywood Broun

Poker is really a generic term for a family of games. The most common variations are:

- Draw Poker
- Five-card Stud
- Seven-card Stud
- Texas Hold 'Em
- Omaha

I will start with how to play draw poker and five-card stud, with particular focus on draw poker, as all other types are derived from these two. If you can master the basics of these two games you can easily adapt to all other forms of poker.

The Basics

Poker is played with between two and twelve people seated at either a circular or a kidney shaped table. A game of poker can last for several hours and is divided into hands. Each hand of poker takes about 3–5 minutes to play, depending on the number of players at the table and how fast they play. Depending on the strength of his/her hand, players make bets by putting money (which is exchanged for chips if you're playing in a casino) into the 'pot'. The objective for each poker player, during a hand, is to win all the money in the pot of each hand. That is, to obtain the highest-ranking hand, or bet out all of the other opponents and be the sole remaining player left in contention. Pots are not all the same size so at the end of the playing session the person who has won the most money is not necessarily the person who has won most pots. The aim of the game is to win as much money during the playing session as possible.

If you are planning to have a social game it is worth setting a limit on the stakes that are to be played for. It is also a good idea to set a finishing time in advance, as the losers, even when playing for very small stakes, usually want to continue playing until they get their money back.

The Ranking of Hands

Although there are many variations of the game of poker, the ranking of hands always remains the same. A poker hand is always made up of exactly five cards. The values of each card from the highest to the lowest are ace, king, queen, jack, 10, 9, 8, 7, 6, 5, 4, 3, 2, ace (an ace can be high or low depending on the circumstance). In the remainder of this book, where appropriate, an ace will be shown as an 'A', a king as 'K', a queen as 'Q' and a jack as 'J'.

Poker hands are ranked in the order of probability of being dealt in five-card combinations from the standard 52-card deck. There are 2,598,960 combinations of five-card hands possible in the standard deck. The number of possible hands in each of the categories is given opposite. You will see that the high card is the commonest hand and easiest to get dealt, hence it is worth the least. By contrast, there are only four combinations of cards which will give a royal flush, making it the rarest hand and hence the most valuable.

Royal Flush • 4
The five highest cards of the same suit. Examples are A♣ K♣ Q♣ J♣ 10♣ or A♥ K♥ Q♥ J♥ 10♥.

Straight Flush • 36
Any five cards of the same suit which are also in sequential order or rank. Examples are 7♦ 8♦ 9♦ 10♦ J♦ or 3♠ 4♠ 5♠ 6♠ 7♠.

Four of a kind • 624
Four cards of the same rank or value. Examples are 10♥ 10♦ 10♠ 10♣ 7♦ or 10♥ 10♦ 10♠ 10♣ K♦. (Again note that all poker hands have five cards.)

Full House • 3,744
Three cards of the same rank or value plus a pair of different rank. Examples are 3♦ 3♠ 3♥ 9♠ 9♦ or J♣ J♦ J♠ 5♠ 5♦.

Flush • 5,108
Five non-sequential cards of the same suit. Examples are A♣ K♣ 7♣ 5♣ 2♣, an ace-high flush, or 10♥ 7♥ 6♥ 4♥ 2♥, a ten-high flush.

Straight • 10,200
Five cards of mixed suits in sequence of rank. An example is 7♦ 8♥ 9♦ 10♦ J♠. Although the ace is normally a high card it can also play as a low card to form a five-high straight (or indeed a straight flush). Thus A♣ 2♥ 3♦ 4♠ 5♠ is the lowest possible straight.

Three of a kind • 54,912
Three cards of the same rank, also called a set or trips (short for triplets). Examples are 6♥ 6♠ 6♦ 10♦ 9♦ or K♥ K♦ K♣ 10♠ 2♠.

Two Pair • 123,552

Any two cards of the same rank, plus any other two cards of the same rank, plus one odd card. Examples are [A♣][A♦] [4♠][4♣] [5♠], called 'aces up' as aces are the higher pair, or [7♦][7♥] [3♦][3♠] [Q♦], called 'sevens up' as sevens are the highest pair.

One Pair • 1,098,240

Any two cards of the same rank, plus three odd cards. Examples are [8♦][8♠] [K♦][J♦][3♠] or [2♥][2♦] [K♦][9♦][7♠].

High Card • 1,302,540

If no player has a pair or better then the highest card held wins. Examples are [A♠][K♠][Q♠][J♠][8♦] which is an ace high, or [9♦][8♥][6♦][4♠][2♦], which is a lowly nine high.

There are some aspects of hand rankings which can be confusing for beginners. For instance, flushes are ordered in terms of their highest card, then the next highest and so on down to the fifth card, so [A♣][K♣][7♣][5♣][3♣] is a bigger flush than [A♦][K♦][6♦][4♦][3♦], although both are called 'ace-high flushes'. Also, if there were two flushes exactly the same size, e.g. [Q♠][7♠][5♠][4♠][2♠] and [Q♣][7♣][5♣][4♣][2♣], the two hands would draw and the pot would be split between both players as in poker there is no difference in the value of suits. Similarly, with two-pair hands, if two players have the same highest pair, the lower pair determines the winner, so A-A-4-4-J would beat A-A-2-2-Q and both would beat Q-Q-J-J-K. In the unlikely event of two players having the same two pair, the player with the higher fifth card would win. Thus, J-J-5-5-Q would beat J-J-5-5-9.

Draw Poker

At the start of the session the players cut the cards to decide who will deal first: the person with the lowest value card is the first to deal. The job of dealer in poker is very important, for not only does he shuffle the deck and deal the requisite number of cards to each player, but he is also in charge of the game during the period of the deal. The dealer will ensure that each player acts in his proper turn and puts the right amount of money into the pot. Play starts with the player on the dealer's immediate left and progresses in a clockwise direction. This means that the dealer enjoys the advantage of being able to bet last. After the first hand has been dealt the role of dealer passes to the player who is sitting on the immediate left of the original dealer and then to each player around the table, again in a clockwise direction, so that all players can enjoy this benefit.

Before the cards are dealt, everyone contributes a small amount to the pot: this is called the ante. This makes sure that there is some money in the pot for the players to fight over at the start of the hand. Once money has entered the pot it can only be taken out again by the winner of that particular hand.

After everyone has anted the dealer shuffles the deck and offers it to the player on his right to cut. Then he deals one card from the top of the deck to each player, starting with the player on his left, dealing clockwise and finishing with himself. He does this five times in all, so that everyone has five cards. It is important that the cards should be cut, because it is one way to reduce the risk of cheating. Sometimes at the start of the session, the players might also cut to determine the seating arrangement, but in most home games people sit where they like at the table. The relative seating positions of players at the table is important for several reasons, some are prosaic but some are tactical. These will be explored later in the chapter on Playing Your Hand.

The Betting

The first player to act in a draw poker game is the one to the immediate left of the dealer. His options are to check (meaning to make no bet at this stage) or open if he likes his cards. To indicate a check, players can say 'check' or simply tap the table. When betting it is usual to announce the amount you are betting, so everyone is clear about what you are doing. Then the option passes to the next player. Once somebody has opened the betting however, those behind can no longer check. They must fold (throw their cards away and take no further part in the hand), call (put in a sum to equal the bet to stay in the game) or raise (increase the bet). So when a player is calling a bet, he puts in the same amount of money as has already been bet. If he is raising he must say 'raise' and put in the amount of money required to call the bet plus an additional amount of money for the raise. Except when a player is 'all-in' (see below for a definition) the amount of his raise must be at least as much as the amount of the bet. So if the bet is £10, the raise must be at least £10. Thus the player making the raise would have to put £20 into the pot, £10 to call the bet and another £10 to raise. All players must have put in the same amount of money in order to stay in the game. In the following example I have kept all of the bets in units of £10, apart from the antes (£1) for simplicity. This would be called a £10 limit game, because the bets are limited to a maximum of £10.

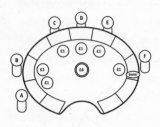

These four diagrams show one complete betting round. At the beginning of the betting round there is £6 in the pot (made up of a £1 ante from each player). The dealer was player F, meaning that player A is first to act. To begin with players A and B both check, player C opens for £10, so now all subsequent players must call this £10, raise or fold. Player D folds and thus takes no further part in this hand. Player E calls by matching the £10 bet. Player F raises £10 and to do this he must first match the £10 bet and then put in a further £10 for the raise, making £20 in all. Note that all players must put an equal amount of money after each betting round to remain in contention for the pot. So as Player F has now put £21 in the pot, players A and B are

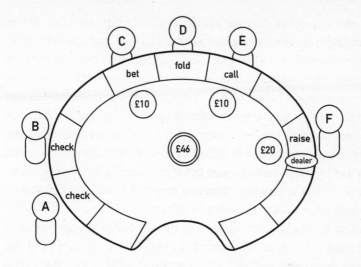

each required to put in £20 (as they have only put in £1 each at this point) in order to stay in the game. However, player C only needs to put in £10 to call (because he has already put in £10). Player A decides to fold, but player B calls the £20. Player C decides to re-raise a further £10, but of course first he puts in the £10 to call, making £20 he puts in at this time. So now all subsequent players must put in the difference to equal the £31 total contribution that

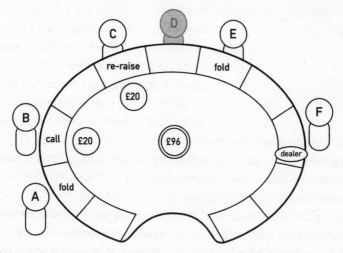

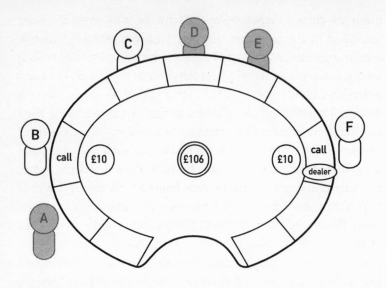

player C has made to the pot. Player E, who would have to put in a further £20, decides this is too expensive and folds, player F calls player C's re-raise of £10, as does player B.

At the end of the first completed betting round then, the action has moved from player A (the player on the dealer's immediate left) to player B then to player C and so on back to player B. The action ends at player B because he is the last to match all of the previous bets and raises. After the betting round there are three players remaining in contention for the pot. They are players B, C and F and they have each contributed £31, including their antes. Player E contributed £11, but has folded giving him no further claim to the money he has already put in the pot, in the same way players A and D have each lost their £1 ante. Therefore at the end of the betting round there is £106 in the pot.

All of this looks complicated on paper, but in reality it is easy to grasp. But be sure you understand how a betting round works, because the same principle applies to all types of poker game.

It is interesting to note that at this stage in the game in the example above, each player has only seen the cards that were dealt to him and can only guess what the other players have. However, there are clues to what a player's hand is, and these clues are identified in the bets that the player makes. Several tentative conclusions can be drawn just from the bets alone in this betting round. Firstly player A had a poor hand, so he initially checked and when later he was faced with a bet he folded his cards. Player B initially checked but then called a bet and a raise and then subsequently he called a re-raise, so he must have liked his hand to some extent. Player C made the first bet, called a raise and made a re-raise of his own, so again he must have liked the hand, possibly thinking it to be the best hand at this stage. Player D folded at the first opportunity, so he most probably had a very poor hand. Player E called the initial £10 bet but none of the subsequent raises, so it is possible that he considered his hand to be of moderate value. Player F called the initial £10 bet and then raised £10, so he must have liked his hand, but he only called player C's final re-raise rather than raising again himself, so he may have had doubts about whether his was the best hand at that stage.

After this first betting round player F, the dealer, then asks the remaining players, starting from the one on his left, how many cards they want to change. By the way, in cases where the dealer has folded early in the progress of the hand, he would still continue with the job of dealing and controlling the action. Remember it is the dealer's job not only to deal the cards, but also to control the action. Each player, when asked, tells the dealer how many cards he wants to exchange. This exchange of cards is called the draw. A player can keep the original five cards, or change up to five (some poker schools allow only a maximum of four to be changed). The dealer exchanges his own cards last and announces how many cards he is changing, e.g. 'dealer takes three'. He makes this announcement so that the other players know how many cards he is exchanging. It is important that every player knows how many cards each other player has exchanged, because this is another way that one gains information on the strength of an opponent's hand. An extreme example to illustrate this point is to consider a player who decides to change none of his cards. You could make the reasonable assumption here that the player had a strong hand (you might also think it was possible that the player could have a weak hand and intended to bluff – but this sort of consideration is left for later in the book). By contrast a player who changes all five cards at the draw will undoubtedly have a worthless starting hand. The cards are dealt from the top of the remaining deck, that is, folded cards are not reincorporated as part of the deck. For this reason, usually draw poker games are limited to seven players to avoid running out of cards. The cards that have been folded are put, by the dealer, into a separate pile beside the pot, and near the centre of the table. These cards are collectively known as the discards or colloquially as 'the muck'. Thus folded cards are said to have been discarded or mucked.

After everyone remaining has exchanged there is another betting round, which proceeds along the same lines as the first, except that the rule is that the player who has opened the betting before the draw always speaks first. At the end of the second betting round, the remaining players show their hands and the person with the best poker hand wins the pot. (This will be the first time in the playing of the hand where players get to see any cards other than their own.) If one player has made a bet that nobody calls, he wins the pot without showing his cards.

In the previous example at the start of the second betting round there is £106 in the pot and the betting might proceed as follows:

Player	B	C	F
Betting Action:		check	bet £10
	fold	raise £10	call £10
Total bet by each player on 2nd round of betting	nil	£20	£20

Here player C was first to act (because he opened the original betting) and checked, player F bet and player B folded, player C then raised, even though he had already checked (this is called a 'check-raise'). Some people consider a check-raise to be unethical and some home games prefer not to allow it, but it is allowed in all games held in casinos. Player F then chooses to call player C's raise although he had the option to raise again. Indeed if both chose to they could have continued raising until one or other ran out of money. Once the last bet or raise made by either player has been called by the other, they then show their hands and the one with the best five-card hand wins the pot, which has now reached £146. This is called the 'showdown'. There are often more than two players involved in a showdown. Note that at any stage if one player makes a bet that the others do not call then that player would win the pot without having to show his cards.

That's the mechanics of the betting dealt with. In the above example, all of the bets were in units of £10 but the limits you place on the game you play is up to you. You might allow units of say £5 before the draw and £10 after or simply allow any amount between £1 and £10 to be bet at any time (but bear in mind that a raise must always be at least as much as the original bet). Usually in a fixed limit game there is a constraint of one bet and three raises per round to prevent two players constantly re-raising each other and trapping a third in between them. To show how this could arise let's look once again at our example. This time the betting proceeds as follows:

Player	B	C	F
Betting Action:		bet £10	call
	raise	re-raise	call
	re-raise	re-raise	call
	re-raise	re-raise	call
	call	call	
Total bet by each player on			
2nd round of betting	£70	£70	£70

Put yourself in the position of player F. It is probable that he would have been happy to just call the first £10 bet and have a showdown. But because the other two players are constantly re-raising each other, player F has to continue to meet the extra bets or fold, losing any chance of winning the hand. On this occasion, player F has had to put in £70, but with the restriction on raising described above, the most he can be forced to put in to have a showdown would be £40, i.e. a bet of £10 and three raises of £10 each. Of course, when only two are left they can raise and re-raise as often as they like.

Sample Hand

Now let's look at a sample draw poker hand from start to finish. In this example, you will be in the privileged position of knowing what all of the players have in their hands. Of course, in a real game you will know for sure only what cards you hold and will have to speculate about the holdings of other players. However, as already stated, there are clues which will give you an indication of the strength of an opponent's hand. Clues already mentioned are the pattern of betting and the number of cards a player exchanges. Other clues can be gleaned from a player's body language (see the chapter on Reading Your Opponent) or from what you know about the player, i.e. what strength of hands he usually plays etc. So let's get on with the sample hand. In this game there are four players (A, B, C, D). Their hands before the draw are:

Player/Hand		Assessment of the hand
A	K♣ 7♦ 5♦ 4♥ 3♠	This is a worthless hand of very low value.
B	2♦ 2♣ 2♥ K♥ 5♠	This hand has three twos which is a very strong starting hand.
C	Q♠ J♠ 9♠ 7♥ 4♠	This hand is only a queen high and hence has no value at this stage. But note that the hand contains four spades. The player could change the 7♥ at the draw and if he got back another spade he would make a flush – a very strong hand. This type of potentially strong hand is called a 'drawing hand'.

D [A♠] [A♣] [8♠] [8♣] [4♣] This hand has two pairs, aces up, which is another very strong starting hand, although on this occasion it is inferior to player B's hand. Incidentally, this hand (aces and eights) is called 'dead man's hand' – see the glossary for an explanation.

Player A is dealer, so player B is first to act and opens for £10. Player C has the drawing hand, so calls the bet. Player D has a very strong starting hand and so he raises £10. It is unfortunate for player D that he does not know what player B is holding, otherwise he would not have raised (indeed he might not even have called). Player A, with his very poor hand, folds. Player B, with a very strong starting hand, re-raises. Player C (with his drawing hand) now has a decision to make: should he call the bet hoping to draw the flush and probably win the pot or should he cut his losses and fold? He knows there is a risk that he will be caught between two players who are re-raising each other so he could lose a lot of money which makes him cautious. On the other hand, he is a player who is at the game to gamble and so he decides to take the risk and call the bet (which is now £20 to him, the £10 raise and the £10 re-raise). He also knows that the one bet and three raises rule applies in this game, so the maximum he would have to put in is £40. Next it is player D who has a decision to make. If he knew for sure that player B had three twos, his correct course would be to fold, but he is not sure. He calculates that player B has a strong hand but it might only be two smaller pairs than he holds. He could re-raise again in this position, but decides that a call is the wisest course.

This leaves three players after the first round of betting, B, C and D. They now have to decide how many cards they should draw. Player B could keep his three twos and draw two cards or keep his three twos and one of the other cards as well and draw only one card. This latter course is what he decides upon, reasoning that by drawing only one card he will make his opponents think that he has only got two pair thus deceiving them about the true strength of his hand. Player C has little choice; he throws the 7♥ away hoping to get a spade. Player D has a choice. He could do the obvious thing by keeping his two pair and taking one card – he would be hoping to draw another ace or an eight, giving him a full house. Alternatively, he could 'stand pat', that is take no cards, again in the hope of disguising the value of his hand. He would be hoping that the other players would think he had a very strong hand indeed and would fold as a result of him making a bet. However, he has seen that the other two players have each drawn one card, so he in turn draws one card because he does not want the other two players to think he has a very strong hand. He wants one or other to call his bet, if he decides to make one.

The cards drawn by each player are as follows:

Player/Cards kept	Cards Drawn	Assessment of the hand
B 2♦ 2♣ 2♥ K♥	5♦	Here player B has thrown away a 5♠, but got back a 5♦. His hand is still strong, but now he feels it can be beaten.
C Q♠ J♠ 9♠ 4♠	9♦	Player C has thrown away a 7♥ but got back a 9♦. His hand is now one pair of nines, not a strong hand.
D A♠ A♣ 8♠ 8♣	6♥	Player D has thrown away the 4♣ but got back a 6♥, again no improvement, but he still has a reasonably strong hand.

In the final betting round, player B is cautious and checks. Player C could bet here trying to make the other players think that he has a strong hand; possibly they might think he has drawn a flush or a straight. If he did bet here the bet would be described as a 'bluff', that is, he would be betting with a weak hand hoping that the other players would fold allowing him to win the pot. However, player C considers that he would not get away with the bluff and also checks. Player D is encouraged by the fact that the other two players have checked. He counts this as a sign of weakness on their part and thinks it is possible that he has the best hand. However, he knows that both of his opponents are capable of checking a good hand in the hope of 'trapping' him and getting him to bet with an inferior holding. Players who use the trapping technique a lot are, not surprisingly, called 'trappers'. So player D decides to be cautious and check. The dealer tells all of the players to turn over their cards and player B wins with the best hand of three twos.

Pot-Limit and No-Limit Games

Most cash games in casinos in the UK are played pot-limit. This means that players can bet up to the amount in the pot. As an example, say five players – A, B, C, D and E – each ante £1, making a total of £5 in the pot. Player A is first on the left of the dealer and opens the betting for £5. Player B calls this £5 and chooses to raise the amount in the pot, which is now £15 (£5 in antes, £5 from player A and the £5 from player B) for a total bet of £20. Player C calls this £20 and raises the amount of the pot again, which is now £50, to make the bet to the next player £70. Player D could then call £70 and raise the pot, which would now be £170 to make the bet a total of £240 to player E. Although this is an extreme example it shows how the amounts in pot limit can increase very quickly. So if you are organising a poker evening at home and don't want anyone to go broke, it's best to stay away from pot limit. This also applies to no-limit betting, the method used in *Late Night Poker*. In no-limit, a player can bet all of the money he has on the table in front of him, at any time, regardless of the pot size.

Going All-in

If at any stage of the hand a player does not have enough money to cover a bet, but nevertheless wants to call, he puts his remaining money in the pot and declares himself to be 'all-in'. Any further bets go into what is called a 'side pot', which the all-in player cannot win. He continues, however, to be in contention for the first pot which is called the 'main pot'. It is not uncommon for a side pot to be bigger than the main pot. Let's have a simple three-player example. There is £100 in the pot and player A bets £20. Player B has only £5 left, so he calls for the £5. Player C also calls but for the original bet of £20. Thus, player B will be in contention for the original £100 in the pot plus his own £5 and £5 from each of the other two players. This makes a main pot of £115 with a side pot of £30. Only players A and C are in contention for the side pot, but all three players are in contention for the main pot.

Five-Card Stud

In this game the dealer gives all the players one card face down and one face up. Each player looks at his own face-down card, usually called the 'hole card', but of course does not know the value of any other player's hole card. Then there is a round of betting after which the players remaining in contention receive a third card face up. Those players folding their hand should do so by turning their face-up card or cards face down. They should be careful not to reveal their hole cards to any other player. This is followed by another betting round and the remaining players receive another card face up (often called an 'up card'). Another round of betting follows. Finally, those surviving the first three betting rounds will receive a last up card. At this point the remaining players will all have one down card (i.e. face down) and four up cards. There is a final round of betting after which each player remaining turns over his hole card and the best hand wins. Of course, if one player bets and all others fold, that player wins the pot without having to show his hole card.

Note that at the beginning of each betting round, the player with the highest up card or cards is the first to act. So, in the first round, if the highest card is, for instance, a king, the person holding the king would be first to bet. (If there is a tie for the high card, the first player on the dealer's left holding the high card would be first to bet because this is the order of play.) On the first betting round only, the high card must make a bet for at least the minimum agreed stake, as a way of getting the game started. On the second and subsequent rounds of betting, the player showing the best hand would be first to speak. For example:

Player:	A	B	C	D
Up cards:	3	J	A	8
	9	J	10	8

Player C acts first on the initial betting round and he must bet at least the minimum bet. On the second round, player B has a pair of jacks showing which is the highest hand and therefore he acts first. He may check or bet. The action then proceeds in the normal clockwise direction.

Notice that in five-card stud there are four betting rounds compared with only two in draw poker. This is worth bearing in mind when organising a game as the pots are likely to be much bigger for stud at the same betting limits.

Sample Five-Card Stud Hand

In this hand, there are four players – A, B, C, D. Player A is the dealer. The stakes in this game are pot limit and each player has anted £1. Once again you are in the privileged position of being able to see all of the players' hole cards, which would not be possible in a real situation. The players hold the following after two cards.

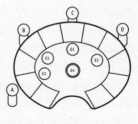

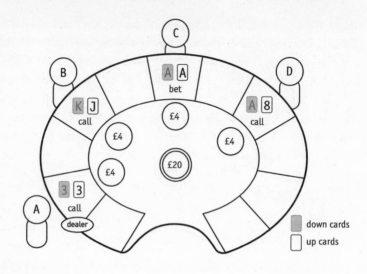

Player:	A	B	C	D
Down card:	3	K	A	A
Up card:	3	J	A	8

Player C has the highest up card so has to bet. He holds two aces which is the highest starting hand. He therefore makes a pot-sized bet of £4. Player D calls with an ace in the hole, player A calls with two 3s and player B calls with two high cards. There is now £20 in the pot.

The second up card is dealt and the hands are now as follows:

Player:	A	B	C	D
Down card:	3	K	A	A
Up card 1:	3	J	A	8
Up card 2:	9	J	10	8

Now player B has the highest up cards so decides to bet the pot. Player C has a choice to make. He does not think that player B has another jack in the hole so is confident that he has the best hand. However, he thinks that if he raises, everyone else will fold and he

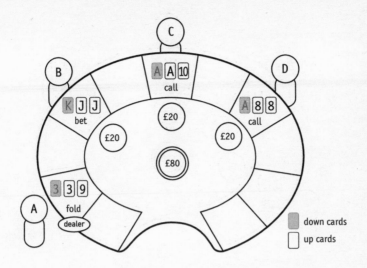

will only win a small pot, so he just calls. Player D also calls with his two 8s; he is hoping to catch another ace giving him two pair. (Notice that it is better for player D to catch an ace than an 8, because, even though three 8s is a better hand than two pair, the three 8s would be in full view of all the other players who would all fold.) Player A decides that his hand is well beaten at this stage and so he folds. It is good tactics in five-card stud to fold if you are 'beaten in sight', that is if the cards you can see the other players holding are better than yours. This leaves three players and there is now £80 in the pot.

The third up card is dealt and the hands are now as follows:

Player:	B	C	D	
Down card:	K	A	A	
Up card 1:	J	A	8	
Up card 2:	J	10	8	
Up card 3:	4	4	K	

Player B still has the highest up cards but is worried about what the other two players hold, so he checks. Player C is still confident that he has the best hand, but he decides not to bet the full amount of

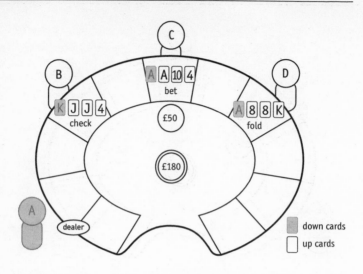

the pot – he only bets £50 – hoping that the other players will call. Player D knows he is beaten by player B and fairly sure he is beaten by player C so, as he did not get the card he wanted, he folds. Player B now thinks that it is a distinct possibility that player C has got two aces, in which case he is beaten so he should fold. However, he knows player C very well and has seen him make a bluff in similar situations in the past. He is also fooled by the fact that player C did not bet the full amount of the pot which he takes as a sign that a bluff is possible. Also player B could still catch a king on the last card and maybe win a very big pot, so he calls. There is now £180 in the pot and the final up card is dealt as follows:

Player:	B	C
Down card:	K	A
Up card 1:	J	A
Up card 2:	J	10
Up card 3:	4	4
Up card 4:	Q	5

Player B is still first to act and makes a snap decision. He quickly decides to bet the size of the pot, that is, £180. He considers that

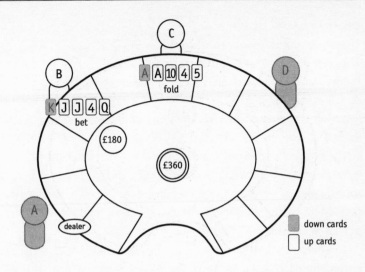

player C might think that he had a Q-J as his starting hand,
meaning that he now has two pair. Player B makes his bet and
instantly regrets his decision because player C looks as if he is
about to call. Then player C hesitates. Of course, he does not know
that he has the best hand, otherwise the correct decision is to raise.
But he knows player B reasonably well (or thinks he does) and
considers that he is not the type of player who bluffs very often. He
therefore wrongly decides that player B probably holds two pair or
conceivably three jacks. After a lot of pondering, player C folds the
best hand. Player B, who has got away with a bluff, breathes a sigh
of relief and wins the pot. Note that if player B's last card had been
a 2 instead of a queen then he would have been less likely to
succeed with the bluff as player C would not then suspect two pair
(i.e. a 4 and a J or a 2 and a J are not likely starting hands for him
to have). By the same token, however, player C is less likely to have
tried the bluff if the final card had been a 2.

Five-card stud can be an interesting game but it can become a
bit stale if everyone plays very conservatively and only enters the
fray with strong starting hands such as an ace or a king as their
hole card or a pair as their first two cards.

Seven-Card Stud

This is a development of five-card stud and generally produces a livelier game. In seven-card stud, the players start with three cards each, two down and one up. Then there is a betting round. Thereafter a further three cards are dealt face up, with a betting round after each. The seventh and last card is dealt face down, and is followed by the final betting round. Players who stay to the last card will have three down cards and four up cards. Seven-card stud has five betting rounds and as a result the pots can be quite large. Rather than playing this game for pot-limit stakes, it is not a bad idea to change to half-pot limit.

In seven-card stud, players use the best five cards, from the seven they are dealt, to make their hand (remember, all poker hands contain only five cards). This means, for example, that a hand containing six hearts would only use the highest five to make the flush. A six-card flush does not beat a five-card flush. Similarly, there is no such hand as three pair. Thus J-J-10-10-4-4-2 would lose to K-K-6-6-Q-7-3.

Texas Hold 'Em

Texas Hold 'Em (usually just called Hold 'Em) is the form played in *Late Night Poker* and is the one most commonly played in casino card rooms. Hold 'Em can be played with only two players or, theoretically, with as many as twenty-two players (this exhausts the number of cards in the deck). In practice, however, it is rarely played with more than twelve players due to the size of the table, with eight to eleven players considered the optimum range.

The first betting round is structured slightly differently from draw or stud. There is usually no ante put in by every player. Instead, the two players on the dealer's left each put in small initial bets, called 'blinds'. These bets are called blind bets (blinds for short) because they are made at a stage before the players receive their cards. As the deal passes round the table a different two players put in (or post) the blinds. Thus over time every player will post the same number of blinds.

In the majority of casino games there is a house dealer, and to ensure that every player has a chance of sitting in what would nominally be the dealer's position a small disk or 'button' is moved around the table. The house dealer always deals the first card to the player on the left of the dealer button. The player with the dealer button is last to act on every round of betting for that hand, with the exception of the first one where the blinds are 'live', meaning that the players who posted the blinds have the option to raise.

The game starts with each player receiving two cards face down. After they have looked at their own cards, there is a round of betting. As the first two players on the dealer's left have put in bets, it is the third player on the dealer's left who is first to act, and because a bet (blind) has already been made he cannot check. He must call the blind, raise or fold. If the action proceeds all the way around to the players who posted the blinds, without being raised, then these players have the option to raise themselves. If they do not wish to do so, they simply say 'no raise' or tap the table.

Once the first betting round is over, the dealer discards (or 'burns') the top card of the deck. It is dealt face down on to the table, this card is called a 'burn card' and it is not used in the play of the hand. This is to ensure that cheating is made difficult or impossible to achieve. If the top card was not burnt then players might be tempted to mark particular cards and try and spot them on top of the deck. If the cards are marked, a player who is able to read the backs will know what the top card is and this information could be very advantageous. For instance, if a player had 6-6 in hand and knew that the first card dealt would be a 6, then that player could bet and raise with impunity.

After the first betting round, three cards are turned face up in the middle of the table. This is called 'the flop'. After a further round of betting, a fourth card, called the 'turn' or 'fourth street' is turned.

Another round of betting is followed by a final face-up card (called the 'river' or 'fifth street'). The five cards in the centre of the table are collectively known as the 'board'. After the last round of betting, the players reveal their hole cards.

Hold 'Em allows a player to use both his hole cards and three from the board, or only one hole card and four from the board, or indeed he can choose not to use any of his hole cards and instead play the five board cards as his hand. This latter case is known as 'playing the board'. Thus, if the board cards were A♣ K♦ Q♦ J♥ 10♠ all the players left in contention would have the highest possible straight (called the top straight) and hence would split the pot between them. Note that in this case there is no flush possible because there would have to be three cards of the same suit on the board. Similarly, for there to be a full house or four of a kind there would have to be at least one pair on the board.

Here is an example:

	Hole Cards	Flop	Fourth Street	Fifth Street
Hand 1	A♥ K♦			
Hand 2	A♣ Q♣	A♠ 9♦ 7♠	Q♦	9♠
Hand 3	7♥ 7♣			
Hand 4	J♠ 10♠			

On the flop, hand 3 is ahead with three 7s (called 'trip 7s'). Hand 1 is second best with two aces and a king as the next highest card (the king in this instance is called the 'kicker'). Hand 2 is third best also with two aces but only with a queen kicker. Although hand 4 is last at this stage the player is not without hope as fourth street could bring a spade card giving a flush or an 8 making a straight. Notice that two of the players are using the same board card (the A♠) as part of their hand which is allowable.

On fourth street, there is minimal change in the order. Hand 3 is still ahead, but now hand 2 is second with two pair and hand 1 is third with one pair. Hand 4 is still last, but now any spade, 8 or king will improve this hand to make it the winner.

On fifth street, all five board cards have now been dealt. Each player can use a combination of the board cards and his own hole cards to make the best five-card combination or hand. In this case, hand 4 has indeed improved to a flush (five spades), but hand 3 has also improved to a full house and wins the pot.

Another example is:

	Hole Cards	Flop	Fourth Street	Fifth Street
Hand	A♣ K♣	K♠ 9♣ 7♠	A♦	3♣

On fourth street, the player can use the A♣ and K♣ from his hand along with the A♦ and K♠ from the board to make two pair but on fifth street he can use the two clubs in his hand and the three clubs on the board to make a flush. Therefore, at various points in the play of the hand, the player used different combinations of cards to make the best five-card poker hand.

Remember that poker is a five-card game, so if the board was 10-10-10-10-3, all players would have four 10s, but the winner of the pot would be the player with the highest hole card. The best possible hand is known as 'the nuts', so if the board was K♥ 6♠ 3♦ 4♥ 10♥ the player holding two hearts, including an ace of hearts would have the nuts and win the pot. But, if the 3♦ were instead a 6♦, this player would no longer have the nuts, since now a full house or four of a kind is possible. Of course, the player might still win the pot with his ace-high flush, but he would not have the nuts.

Omaha

The rules of Omaha are identical to those of Hold 'Em except that each player receives four hole cards instead of two and each player must use exactly three board cards and two hole cards to make the hand. This second difference can be confusing for beginners and players who are used to Hold 'Em. These examples show how it works:

Hole Cards	Flop	Fourth Street	Fifth Street
A♣ K♣ J♠ J♥	K♦ K♥ Q♦	9♥	9♣

Best Hand

The hole card K♣ makes trip kings but note that this player does not have a full house. This would require the use of only one hole card and four board cards, or three hole cards and two board cards, which are prohibited combinations.

Hole Cards	Flop	Fourth Street	Fifth Street
A♣ 2♥ Q♠ J♠	A♦ K♣ 3♣	9♣	10♣

Best Hand

This player's best hand is the ace-high straight using the Q♠ J♠ hole cards and A♦ K♣ 10♣ from the board. Note that he does not have a flush as this would require the use of only one hole card and four from the board.

Hole Cards	Flop	Fourth Street	Fifth Street
A♣ K♥ Q♥ J♥	4♠ 4♥ 4♦	4♣	Q♣

Best Hand

Here a beginner might think that he has four of a kind with an ace as the kicker. Alternatively, he might think that he has a full house of three 4s and two queens. But neither of these hands is allowed because in each case he is using only one hole card. The highest hand this player can have is three 4s with an ace and a king as kickers. The nuts in this example would be where a player holds two queens in hand, making a full house of three queens and two 4s.

Playing Your Hand

The race is not always to the swift, nor the battle to the strong; but that's the way to bet.
Damon Runyon

In the last chapter we examined five variations of poker. However, from here on we will focus only on Hold 'Em poker as it is the most commonly played game in the UK and it is the game featured in *Late Night Poker*. Once again, note that the lessons learned from reading about the strategies involved in playing Hold 'Em, which are discussed here, can be applied to other forms of the game.

In this chapter, I shall be looking at how to play the first two cards in Hold 'Em, play after the flop and finally play on fourth and fifth streets. The first and most important decision you will have to consider is – should I play this hand at all? So let's start with the first two cards.

The First Two Cards

Hold 'Em, like five-card stud (now rarely played), offers the player only two cards before he has to make his first decision. Seven-card stud offers three, Omaha four (at least – some forms give five or even six cards), and, in the granddaddy of them all, draw poker, you see five cards before you have to make a decision. However, in Hold 'Em we need only worry about the first two cards. The number of different combinations of two-card hands is really quite small. For this reason, most poker books offer tables detailing every possible combination and what to do with it. I don't intend to follow that route here because I consider it to be of limited value to learn a table by rote. In any case, many of these hands have been subject to endless debate in technical circles ever since the first hand rankings appeared in David Sklansky's seminal work *Hold 'Em Poker* in 1976. (See Bibliography.) So here are some general tips.

Pairs

These are valuable holdings and are always tempting to play. You'll see a pair about once in every sixteen hands so they have considerable scarcity value. A lowly pair of 3s may not look much, but it's a big hand if the flop comes an innocuous looking K-6-3. If somebody has made two kings, possibly holding A-K, you're going to get plenty of action against your trip threes. So pairs are often worth playing because, if you are lucky enough to flop trips, it will be very hard for your opponents to know that you have made a strong hand.

However, small pairs (8s and below) can become an expensive drain on your bankroll if you are continually putting in a lot of money to see the flop (i.e. call the bet to stay in the game and 'see' what the flop will bring). Since a pair will make trips on the flop only about one time in eight (7/1 odds), it can seem a very long time between payoffs.

Medium pairs have more value because there is the chance that the flop will come with no high cards, giving you a strong hand. For example, two 9s are good if the flop is 8-7-3. Here you would have what is referred to as an 'overpair', as your pair is bigger than the highest card on the flop. But remember that it is very much odds against getting a low flop like this one.

Here's a helpful mental guide for evaluating pairs. Aces, kings and queens are big pairs. Jacks, 10s and 9s are medium pairs. Anything below is a small pair. This might help you to not get too carried away with a pair of jacks, one of the classic trap hands in Hold 'Em. Supposedly, in the old days in Texas, if an opponent claimed he had 'a small pair' it was kings. The point being made, and only half in jest, is that some players consider only A-A to be a big pair, all other pairs being small.

Ace-High Kicker

Starting cards of an ace with a high kicker (i.e. A-K, A-Q, A-J, A-10) are the bread-and-butter Hold 'Em hands that win a lot of pots. Most of them are playable, especially if they are suited, but nevertheless they require caution when considering the kicker. Ace-king is playable in almost all occasions. If you flop an ace or a king, it must be the top pair and it must be the best kicker.

However, ace-queen is troublesome. A classic situation is where a player raises and you call with ace-queen. The flop comes with an ace and two 'rags' (small or useless cards). If your opponent bets out again, what do you do? If he has ace-king, things are bleak for you. You must hit your queen to win. In fact, Doyle Brunson, who was world champion in 1976 and 1977, has said that he considers ace-queen just about his least favourite hand. Ace-jack and ace-10 are easier to 'get away from' if an ace flops because it is more likely they will be beaten.

Ace-Small Kicker (Ace-9 and Below)

This is about the only hand where being suited is a significant advantage. Ace-4 of hearts could win a big pot; king-4 of hearts could just as easily lose one. That is, with an ace-4 of hearts and three other hearts on the flop (or board) you can always be confident that you have the top flush, but with a king-4 there is a chance that your opponent will have the ace-high flush. In this case you are liable to lose all of your money.

All players have some flaws in their game and my worst is to play ace-small suited too often. The fact is, if an ace comes, you can't be certain you've got the best hand, and if two of your suit come, you're still about a two-to-one underdog to make your flush. Nevertheless, this is one of the few hands, when on occasion the flush does come, where you can move your chips to the centre, confident that you have the nuts.

Ace-small kicker unsuited is a trash hand in a full game. Nevertheless, this doesn't stop many people playing it. However, in a short-handed game, especially in the latter stages of a tournament (a full explanation of tournament play is provided in Chapter 8), it becomes worth a lot more.

Two Cards 10 or Higher

These are hands such as king-queen, king-jack, queen-jack, jack-10 etc. Indiscriminate play of these hands will cost you a lot of money in the long run. King-queen suited is a lot better than king-10 offsuit, but a lot of players treat them as virtually the same hand. King-queen gives you two chances to flop top pair whereas king-10 gives you only one chance. In addition, if you flop a pair of kings to your K-10 you cannot be confident about your kicker. Much as Doyle Brunson hates ace-queen, I hate king-10 (and king-9). I lost a number of big pots when I first went to Las Vegas before I realised how bad they can be.

I would rather have a jack-10 suited than a king-10 offsuit in most situations because you'll probably get into less trouble! Of course, in a short-handed game this is not necessarily the case, as, if you are contesting a pot with a small number of players, high cards tend to dominate. The reasoning here is that if you hold a king and a jack as your starting cards and there are nine other players, you are very unlikely to hold the best hand. But if you hold same king and jack against only one other player, the chances od that you have the best hand.

Straight and Flush Cards

Every time you play a 10-9 of diamonds or a 6-4 of spades, you are silently willing the words 'flush' or 'straight' as the dealer turns the flop. Sadly, these desires rarely materialise but when they do, you can be handsomely rewarded. But are they always worth playing?

Against a number of players, possibly. For example, if you are sitting on the button with something like a 9-8 suited, and there has been a raise and two calls before the action has reached you, you might consider taking the flop (i.e. calling to stay in the game). There is plenty of money in there already and you have a chance of winning a big pot. But don't take this too far. Don't use the excuse that two players have already called to justify putting your money in with say, a 10-5 suited. It's just not worth it. And, similarly, if there is a raise and no callers before your turn to act, most, if not all, of these hands should be folded! You're just too far behind and there's not enough incentive.

Worthless Starting Hands

Basically, everything not covered already falls into this category. Such hands as J-5 offsuit or a 4-2 are total garbage and should not be played.

Position

Position means how far round the table you are in relation to the dealer. The nearer the dealer you are (on the dealer's right), the better off you are. The dealer has the best position of all as he gets to act last on each betting round (except the first).

Having to act first is a major disadvantage in Hold 'Em. Say you have raised with an ace-jack, and have hit nothing on the flop.

What do you do if you are first to speak? If you bet out, you take the risk of being raised by those behind you who have made good hands. If you check, those behind may bet forcing you to fold. However, if you had that same ace-jack on the button things are very different. If you make a strong hand, you are forcing the others to 'bet into you' (i.e. bet before your turn to act) and if you flop nothing, and somebody bets, you can then pass, risking nothing.

Generally then, the earlier your position, the better your hand needs to be before you should enter the fray. In a tough game, with many people raising before the flop, expect to 'pass' (i.e. fold) nearly all your hands in the first two seats in a full game. Ace-jack and ace-10 offsuit, for example, are definite non-starters here. As are ace-small suited and small pairs (say 6s and below). If you call with two 6s and somebody raises you, what do you do? If you call him, you are seven to one against to make trips on the flop. Anything else and you'll have to check (unless you attempt a bluff), thus handing the initiative to your opponent! He does not even need a pair to bet. He has position and this is all that is needed.

If you do call with, say, ace-jack suited or ace-queen, in an early position, and a solid player raises you, I would recommend folding because there are too many uncertainties. If an ace comes, do you bet into him or not? He might have ace-king. Better not to get into this dilemma in the first place. I am not advocating tight or conservative play here, just solid, sensible play, which is something completely different.

The Flop and Beyond

The person who invented Hold 'Em came up with a fantastic idea in deciding that the first three cards should be dealt at the same time. This means that the flop is the defining moment in the hand. In five- or seven-card stud, where cards are dealt one at a time, the value of your hand changes slowly. In Hold 'Em, a strong hand before the flop can be made almost worthless on the flop, while an innocuous-looking hand before the flop can turn into a monster. Hence the expression often heard around Hold 'Em tables, 'any two cards can win'. So, 7-deuce? (Deuce is a term for 2.) No problem, but only if the flop comes 7-7-deuce. In reality, any two cards can win, but it is much more likely that A-A will win than say 7-4 and it is on the likelihood or chance of a win that you risk your money.

What to Do after the Flop's Out

1. If you have nothing, get out.

This simple rule will save you a lot of money over your poker-playing lifetime. But a lot of players violate it. If you have queen-jack of hearts, a good starting hand, and the flop is the king of diamonds, and the 6 and 3 of spades, get out. Throw your hand away and wait for the next hand.

2. If you don't have much, get out.

This is a harder rule to follow than the previous one but it'll probably save even more money. For example, you have a 9♦ 8♦ and the flop is Q♣ 8♥ 3♦, i.e. all of different suits (called a 'rainbow flop'). The optimist in this position sees a pair and a back door flush draw (see Glossary). But if someone bets the pot, representing a pair of queens, or better, where are you? You need to hit a 9 or an 8 for an immediate improvement, which still may not win. If a diamond comes, that gives you a four flush, but your opponent, if he's a quality player, is likely to bet the pot again. Do you want to call a pot-size bet with only one card to come? I suggest not.

After the flop, you have seen five cards out of seven or 70 per cent of your hand. It is usually a weak play to call on the flop, only to pass on fourth street if there's another bet.

As a general rule, then, inside straight draws, back door flush draws, second or third pair, or even top pair with a weak kicker, are better off in the muck (that is, you are better to pass them). Of course, if you have a strong suspicion your opponent may not have a solid hand or is attempting a bluff, that's a different matter.

David Sklansky introduced the concept of semi-bluffing into the language of poker and it is now part of the lexicon of table talk. This is a hand that you are betting with which you hope will not be called, but if it is called, still has a chance to win. So, in the hand above, for example, you might bet your pair of 8s as a semi-bluff if your opponent checks to you, showing weakness. You hope he folds, but if he doesn't, you still have a number of ways to win. This is better than a pure bluff, where you have no hand at all. If your opponent calls in the latter case, you know for sure you have lost your chips. Note that a semi-bluff, by definition, can only be made if there are still cards to come, as you are hoping your hand will improve.

3. If you've hit something, and you like it, bet it.

Say you've played a small pair and now you've hit trips. You should usually bet here. For example, if you've played pocket 4s (two 4s in the hole), and the flop comes 10-9-4, I would definitely bet. This applies particularly if two suited cards come on the flop which means somebody might have a flush draw. If you checked this type of hand and the next card is, say, the jack of the same suit, your three 4s don't look so good any more (the jack could have made your opponent a flush or a straight). It's always tempting, when you flop a big hand, to check and hope somebody else bets, or check and hope somebody catches something on fourth street that gets them involved. But unless you are against a very aggressive player, who nearly always bets if he is checked to, it is usually safer to bet to protect your hand. If you get raised, of course, you have to re-evaluate your hand – it might be second best, but don't let the fear of being raised stop you from betting.

More About Big Pairs

Aces, kings and queens before the flop, although great to have, can sometimes present problems in terms of playing them optimally. Queens in particular are another classic Hold 'Em trap hand which many inexperienced players tend to overplay. If another player raises before the flop, it is OK to call with two queens, but re-raising is asking for trouble in a pot-limit or no-limit game. If the raiser has aces or kings, you are a big underdog, and if he has ace-king, a likely hand for him, you are only a slight favourite. In a tournament, if you were down to a short stack (i.e. had very little money or chips left) or your opponent had a short stack, re-raising wouldn't be wrong, but I don't encourage it. (The importance of stack size as a factor in your decision-making thought processes is considered in more detail in the chapters on Reading Your Opponent and Tournaments.) Everything I have said about queens applies with even more emphasis to a pair of jacks. Those players who are desperate to get all their money in before the flop with a pair of jacks are putting their bankroll in serious jeopardy.

Kings are safer, but can still be a tricky hand to play. A raise from another player normally merits a re-raise to shut out the rest of the field but what if he then raises again? Unless he is a maniac, he probably has aces, or maybe ace-king. If you are playing a tournament, especially a freeze-out tournament, it is questionable play to commit all your money early on before the flop with two kings against an all-in raiser.

My own experience of holding two kings has been mixed. Four times in two years in tournaments and cash games, I re-raised with two kings and was immediately re-raised. None of my opponents were particularly tricky players. In each case, I was about 90 per cent sure I was up against pocket aces. But two kings is a tough hand to throw away. All four times, I called, against my better judgement, and each time my opponents had aces. Of course, maybe I'm just unlucky. You sit there all night never being dealt two cards that hang together. Finally, after four hours, two kings come along. You raise, he re-raises. You put all your money in and, sure enough, you end up looking at two aces.

So it is an option to pass or fold two kings, just don't tell anybody you're doing it! Just throw them in quietly without making a fuss. If you show your hand to your opponent, you are telling him that you are giving credit for aces, which he might not have had. Also, the other players at the table might think you are playing too cautiously or conservatively (to use poker vernacular, 'too tightly') and start bluffing you out of pots.

What about aces? It is wonderful to be dealt A-A as your two hole cards, but do you put all your money in or not? Remember that, in a tournament, staying in is the most important thing, so I'd be more inclined to play A-A aggressively. For example, if one player raises and another calls, I would almost always re-raise, but against only one player, I'd be more tempted to just call, which is a deceptive play and will lead your opponent to think you have a lesser hand. Aces usually want only one player to play against. If you're against three or four, there is every chance one of these players will hit something on the flop to beat you.

Some of the best players I've seen are players who have just called with aces behind a raiser. They are hoping the raiser gets a little help on the flop. Say he might have a king-queen. If a king or a queen comes on the flop, the raiser will probably bet. The player can now raise with the A-A and hopefully win a big pot. If the player had re-raised immediately before the flop, the original raiser (if he's a half-decent player) would probably have thrown his hand away.

The drawback here, of course, is that the original raiser might get too much help on the flop and hit the front. If the flop came king-queen-three, in the above example, probably only a world-class player would be able to get away from A-A without serious damage.

But really the main 'purpose' of having two aces in Texas Hold 'Em is to have them beaten, so that you can have a 'good' hard luck story (called a 'bad beat story') to tell your fellow players at the bar.

Good Flops to Your Hand

Your Hand	Flop
K♣ K♥	Q♦ 6♥ 3♠

Any time you have an overpair to the flop it is usually favourable. You should get plenty of action from anyone holding a queen with a good kicker. The only real danger on this flop is trips. If somebody raises you, it's a judgement call on your part which of the two they have – queen with good kicker or trips.

Your Hand	Flop
8♦ 8♥	K♥ 8♠ 3♠

This is an excellent flop. Only three kings beat you at this stage. If somebody has three kings, there's really nothing you can do except lose your money. Only world champions are capable of throwing away middle set in Texas Hold 'Em. If someone bets, raise. If you bet and are raised, you might as well put all your money in and hope they put theirs in. If they've got a flush draw, you're about a 3 to 1 favourite to win. Good luck.

Your Hand	Flop
A♠ K♠	A♥ 8♦ 3♠

Any flop to ace-king containing either an ace or a king is generally favourable. If you bet in this example, many players with A-Q or A-J (or even A-10 or A-9) will raise, giving you an ideal opportunity to get all your money in with only a slim chance of being outdrawn. The main danger here is somebody playing an A-3 suited or an A-8 suited. Since a lot of players will play any ace, you'll often run into two pair. Remember also that whenever an ace flops, there's always a chance of a straight on the next card. (This is because the ace plays at the high and low end of a straight. If you don't believe me, put out a flop containing an ace and any two random cards. You can always find a card that will complete a straight). So, in general, play your hand strongly to discourage people drawing against you.

Your Hand	Flop
K♠ Q♠	Q♦ 9♠ 5♠

Here you have top pair with a good kicker and a king-high flush draw. Although you don't have the best possible kicker, or the best draw, because you have both covered you can never be drawing dead. In other words, if somebody is playing against you with the ace-flush draw, you don't want a spade to fall, but your queens are winning. On the other hand, if someone has ace-queen or trips, you are behind, but you have a lot of cards that can win the pot for you.

This two-way hand illustrates a general principle. If you are considering committing all your chips (in a tournament or cash game) try to pick a spot where, if you are behind, you still have a fair chance to win. A good example for *not* committing all of your chips would be the following:

Your Hand	Flop
A♠ A♣	9♦ 8♦ 7♦

If an opponent bets into you here, what should you do? If it were for my whole stack, I would pass. It's true you may be ahead. He may have only the bare ace of diamonds, or a hand like 10-9, giving him a pair and straight draw. In these cases, you still have a good chance to win. However, if he has a flush or a jack-10 for a straight, you are almost dead. In a situation where you are either slightly ahead or way behind, pass. It doesn't matter that you've got pocket aces which are the very best starting hand you can get, just pass them – it's allowed.

Your Hand	Flop
6♠ 5♠	J♥ 5♦ 5♣

Here you've flopped the bottom two pair. This is probably winning, but you must play your hand on the flop. If there's a bet, that player probably has a jack or an overpair. You're winning, so get your money in. The worst thing that can happen to your hand is for another jack to fall on fourth street. If that happens, your two pair are worthless (actually you've got three pair) and, if there's a bet, you must pass. In addition, any connecting card to the jack (8 through queen) is dangerous as is an ace. So raise and hope your opponent passes. If your opponent does call and one of these cards falls on fourth street, be careful – your opponent *may* have made two pair.

Your Hand	Flop
A♠ 10♠	10♦ 10♥ 3♣

This is a big flop to your hand. You have trips with the best kicker and it is very unlikely that a player will have stayed with a 10-3. Hopefully, you'll get action from somebody with K-10, J-10 etc. Few players will lay down the other 10 in these circumstances and you have little chance of being outdrawn. Your only real worry is somebody with pocket threes who has turned what is described as the 'underfull' (full house to the lowest card on the flop). If that happens there is not much you can do about it, so it's back to the drawing board.

Playing Draws

Note that in all the hands we looked at above, you flopped something tangible to your hand – trips, two pair, or just one pair. What about when you flop a draw? By a draw, I mean a hand that could turn into something big on the last two cards but at the moment doesn't amount to much. These hands are very tricky to play. A lot of players get busted out of tournaments on a draw when, probably, they shouldn't be playing them. As T J Cloutier, the prolific US tournament winner, says, 'Draws are death'.

Let's look at a typical layout where you might consider playing a draw.

Your Hand	Flop
J♥ 10♥	K♦ 7♥ 3♥

If a solid player bets the pot and everyone passes to you, should you call? We've all done it, but the answer is no, definitely not. Your opponent is a solid player, so give him credit for a pair of kings (any pair is in front of you at this point anyway). You must hit one of nine hearts to make your flush. In other words, you are about a 4/1 underdog to make it on the next card. If a heart does come, your opponent may well stop betting, since he must fear the possibility of a flush. If it doesn't, he will likely bet the pot again. Do you want to call again with one card to come?

What if another player called in between you and the bettor? Some players now get it into their heads that they have 'value' but do they? Remember that your flush draw is only jack high. If somebody is playing a higher flush draw you may end up making your hand only to find out it is second best. The same applies if there is a pair on the flop. You can make your hand and lose to a full house. There's little sense, in my view, in committing money with a draw that you can't be sure will win.

There are some exceptions when you might want to play your draw in a tournament.

1. **You're short stacked**. In this case, you've just got to put your money in and hope. If you are all in on the flop, at least you will get two cards for your money.

2. **Your opponent is short stacked.** In this case, gambling with a draw isn't so bad because you know, once your opponent is all in, it can't cost you any more.

3. **The initial bet is very small.** In a low ante game, if all the players have plenty of money, you can even call on the flop with something like this layout:

Your Hand	Flop
10♠ 8♠	9♦ 6♣ 4♥

If a 7 comes on fourth street, you have the nuts and hopefully someone who turned another good hand such as trips on the flop will not be able to get away from the hand.

I must admit I do loosen up when it comes to the nut-flush draw. You know you'll win if it hits (providing a pair doesn't come) and it also has the added value that pairing the ace might win on its own.

That's all I've got to say about draws. It's boring not playing them but that's how the top players take down the money in the big tournaments (so I'm told!). But if you want to play them, play them aggressively. Raise all-in on the flop. A draw has a lot more value with two cards to come than with one, and there's a fair chance your opponent will be too terrified to call, but pick your spot. There's no point in putting all your chips in with a draw against a player who only worries about what he has and pays no attention to what his opponent might have. Against these types, you'll be called and you'll have to hit your hand.

Fourth and Fifth Street Play

Perhaps surprisingly, there is not a lot to say here. If you have taken on board everything I have said about play on the flop, then you shouldn't be in with a marginal hand. If you were betting with top pair, did not get raised and fourth street looks favourable, go ahead and bet again.

Be more worried about flush cards than overcards. For example, if you had A-10, the flop was 10♥ 6♠ 3♠, you bet and were then called by one opponent, you would feel reasonably comfortable with top pair and top kicker. If fourth street brings a K♦ you need not be too worried about this overcard, as the only hand you would have to fear your opponent holding is K-10, which is not too likely. You might be more inclined to fear an overpair such as J-J. Nevertheless, if you are checked to, you should consider betting as your opponent is showing weakness by the check.

If, however, fourth street brings a spade then you have to be extremely careful as a flush is a likely holding for your opponent. If your opponent checks, be cautious and check yourself – he might be slow-playing the flush. If you are first to act then again take the cautious approach and check. Your opponent must also be fearful of a flush if he does not hold one himself. So give him some credit if he bets because now all you can beat is a bluff. If he is a tricky player you might suspect a bluff, but it is going to cost you to find out. So in this type of situation it is often best just to give your hand up. Remember it is only good players who can be bluffed, so if your opponent does show down a bluff after you have passed the winner, just mark it down to experience. Believe me you will feel more of a fool if you call one or more bets and he shows you a flush. You'll be asking yourself for the next half dozen hands why you called when you knew there was a flush out there.

Drawing Hands

If the position is reversed and it is you that has the drawing hand which has come good on fourth street, you have the choice of whether to bet out or to check and try to trap your opponent. In a tournament, if I was short stacked, I would probably bet as I wouldn't want to risk being outdrawn. But in a cash game, particularly if I hit the nut flush, I would be inclined to check hoping to elicit a bluff or trap my opponent into thinking I do not have the flush. Straights are more vulnerable so I would be much less inclined to slow play a straight. It is appropriate here to give a word of caution about straights. If you have the ignorant end of the straight you need to exercise circumspection. For example, if you have 7♦ 6♠ and the flop and fourth street bring 9♦ 8♠ 4♣ 10♠, you have the lowest possible straight (ignorant end). It is probably a winner but your opponent could have the Q-J. Much less likely is the J-7 as not too many players will be in with this sort of hand. In Hold 'Em it is still OK to bet the bottom end of the straight, but it is a recipe for disaster in Omaha.

Fifth Street

If you get as far as fifth street ('the river'), remember there is now much less cause to bet. You no longer need to bet to protect your hand as all of the cards are out. Most large bets on the river are therefore from big hands or are bluffs. Most players, for example, will not bet top pair top kicker on the river, because it is too likely to be beaten if called. A player who has been betting all of the way, but then checks on the river, probably has a medium-strength hand which he wants to show down for nothing. Nevertheless, I would not recommend a bluff here. If you have got nothing, just accept your fate as a bluff is too likely to be called.

So here we end the strategy section. You are now equipped with everything you need to become a world champion. Except, that is, for expert card- and people-reading skills, full working knowledge of poker odds, the courage to put all of your chips in the pot on a complete bluff, endless patience, years of experience and the little matter of the $10,000 entry fee.

Probability

Probability means the chance or likelihood of something happening. It's a big word, with too many syllables to pronounce after a long night in the bar. So what's it all about? How much do you need to know?

Well, you don't need to go to the lengths of sitting with a calculator at the table in order to be a winner at the game. But a basic grounding in odds is no bad thing. It might stop you from making some big mistakes at the poker table.

Here's an example:

Your Hand	Flop	Your Opponent's Hand
A♠ 6♠	Q♠ 7♠ 2♣	K♥ K♦

Suppose you and your opponent put all your money in and turn your cards over. What are the chances of you winning the pot? To figure this out, look at the number of cards that can win for you. There are nine spades (for a flush) and three aces (for a pair of aces). That's a total of twelve 'outs' (a card that wins for you is called an 'out'). So, since you've got two cards to come that makes a total of 24 winners. That's over half the deck remaining, so you must be favourite!

Well, no, not quite. You can't just take your number of outs and double them because if both cards are winners, you don't get paid twice. The correct way to figure the problem is to say 'the only way I can lose is if I miss twice in a row'. What are the chances of that happening? Well, on fourth street, you have 33 losers from the 45 cards remaining in the deck, and if you miss that, there are 32 losers left for fifth street from the 44 cards now remaining in the deck. So the chance of you missing is:

$$\frac{33}{45} \times \frac{32}{44} = 0.53$$

Since the probability (chance) of you missing twice is 0.53, the probability of you succeeding at least once (i.e. making your hand) is 0.47 or 47 per cent.

Of course, you won't win 47 per cent of the time because your opponent can improve as well. For example, you might hit the [A♥] on fourth street only for your opponent to make three kings with the [K♣] on the river.

So here are the chances of you improving your hand in some common Hold 'Em situations:

Flush	Board	Top Set
[A♥] [Q♥]	[9♥] [7♥] [3♥]	9-9

The set of 9s (or trips) must see a pair on the board to win. The chance of this is about 33 per cent. So, if somebody with a made flush bets the pot and sets you all in for your whole stack, purely on the odds, it's not a bad play to call, since you are getting the correct pot odds. Of course, you might not want to do it in a tournament, since you'll be out if you don't make it.

Flush	Board	Top Two Pair
[A♥] [Q♥]	[9♥] [7♥] [3♥]	9-7

Here the two pair is in much worse shape. The two pair is about 5/1 against to fill up.

Straights against trips and two pair are more or less the same odds as for flushes, so I won't duplicate the calculations here.

Trips	Flop	Flush Draw
6-6	[K♦] [6♥] [3♥]	[K♥] [J♥]

This is another common match up (this example is from the final of series two of *Late Night Poker*). The flush player can expect to see a heart about one third of the time but it won't always win because the trips can turn into a full house (as happened to Devilfish – see chapter on Analysis of Hands). Overall, trips are a 3 to 1 favourite against the flush draw.

A straight draw against trips has about the same chance. An overpair against a board pair is:

Overpair	Flop	Pair
K♥ K♣	Q♦ 6♣ 3♠	A♠ Q♠

Here the pair can hit an ace or a queen to win. Note also that there is one spade on the flop, so the A♠ Q♠ can win with a 'backdoor' flush (two running spades on fourth and fifth streets). Here, the overpair of two kings is about a 3.5 to 1 favourite.

Pair	Flop	Flush Draw/Overcard
K♥ K♦	Q♠ 7♠ 2♣	A♠ 6♠

We have looked at this one already. The two kings are favourite but not by much (about 5/4). Now what about a pair verses a straight and a flush draw:

Pair	Flop	Straight and Flush Draw
A♥ 5♥	A♦ 9♣ 8♣	J♣ 10♣

This is one of the few times when the draw in Hold 'Em is actually the favourite. Although the two aces are nominally in front, the draw has fifteen cards to win with and will improve slightly over half the time.

Pair	Flop	Straight and Flush Draw with Overcards
A♥ 9♥	9♣ 8♣ 3♦	J♣ 10♣

This is the same as the previous example, but now the draw has two overcards to beat the pair of 9s, and will win the pot about two times out of three. The annoying thing is, of course, that this still leaves one time out of three when you will miss your draw completely. If you get all your money in with this sort of hand be prepared for some major disappointments.

That's enough about play on the flop. What about before the flop?

Your Hand   Your Opponent's Hand

K♥ K♦   A♠ A♣

This is bad news. You basically need a king to win (although you might nick it with a very lucky flush). You're about 4/1 the underdog.

Your Hand   Your Opponent's Hand

A♣ K♣   Q♥ J♥

You are favourite but not by as much as many people seem to think. Your opponent can hit a pair, straight, or flush to win. He'll win slightly more than one time in three, that is, odds of about 2/1 against.

Your Hand   Your Opponent's Hand

A♠ K♦   A♥ Q♥

Better. Your opponent needs to see a queen (and no king) or a flush. The A-K is about a 5 to 2 favourite.

Your Hand   Your Opponent's Hand

A♠ K♠   2♥ 2♦

This is the all time classic Hold 'Em match up. You see it time and time again in tournaments. Basically, it's even money. A coin toss.

The pair has more chance the higher it is because of the possibility of the board coming two pair, e.g. in the above situation the board might come J-10-10-6-6. Thus a pair of deuces would be losers, but 7s would be winners. But even two queens are only about 6 to 5 favourite against A-K. To win a tournament, you've got to get lucky and that means surviving your fair share of coin-toss situations.

Rules & Etiquette

The minute you start talking about what you are going to do if you lose, you have lost.
George P Shultz

Rules

One of the great problems of playing poker is that there is not as yet a standardised set of rules. There seems to be a slightly different set of rules existing in every casino. There does not even seem to be consistency across the same casino chains and for casinos in the same geographic area. However, because it would take up considerable space, I will not attempt to give a detailed listing of rules. You would be well advised however to check the rules in every casino you attend and not assume that because there is a rule in your normal club that this will apply in another. Disputes at the poker table are another big problem. What I would like to do here is to set out some general rules and suggested rules which might be helpful for players to use as guidelines in the event of a dispute.

The sit-down, buy-in-for-cash games should apply to a player's initial and subsequent rebuys if all that player's chips are lost. Players buying in short (i.e. for less than the minimum) are the cause of many card room disputes. The player can sit down with any amount of money, no matter how much, as long as it is at least the minimum buy-in. A player with chips may add additional chips to his stack as he desires when not involved in a pot, but may not take chips off the table until quitting the game. Chips and/or money should be in clear view of every player and a player has the right to ask an opponent how much he is playing and to be told. Hidden cash, such as under a cigarette packet or ashtray, cannot be bet. Money and/or chips from the table are not allowed to be transferred from one player to another (this makes collusion more difficult).

If a player returns to the game after an absence of less than two hours it should be considered part of the same playing session and therefore the player must put down the same number of chips he left the table with. This would stop players winning heavily, leaving the table and coming back a short time later with the minimum buy-in again. Arguably this practice causes more disputes in card rooms than any other single issue.

Chips from the table can be used to pay for items such as drinks or food and for tipping waitresses, but they should not be used for side bets outside the game. Examples of such side bets are who will win the next pot, who will have the highest card in hand etc. These types of bets slow up the game and are irritating for other players.

A player is responsible for the protection of his own hand. A player has no remedy if his hand becomes mucked by contact with discards or is accidentally taken in by the dealer. A player facing a bet who discards his hand may not reclaim it. However, a player who discards his hand when not facing a bet may reclaim the hand if it has not touched the muck.

It is, therefore, most important to be responsible for your own hand and not to muck it until you are sure you cannot win. A player can only contest the pot while he is still in possession of his hand. My suggested rule is that a hand folded and turned up by someone other than the owner of the hand is a dead hand. It is the dealer's role to muck and turn discarded hands. The dealer may not show the hand of an absent player only the player may show down a live hand and claim the pot. A hand exposed by one player to another when heads up is not a folded hand. The hand is only dead when the owner folds it and the dealer kills it (by touching it to the discards).

A player is not allowed to make a string bet. This is a bet (or often a feigned bet) which could be used to gauge an opponent's reaction. The bet is almost made and then can be increased or decreased in amount depending on the opponent's reaction. It is a bet that can initially look like a call, but then turns into a raise or a fold. To avoid this happening to you accidentally, I advise that you announce the amount of your bet before you make it. In the same vein a player who calls a bet without indicating that a raise is to follow may not then raise the pot.

In tournament play, deals are permitted between players if they are announced. It happens anyway, so why not make a virtue out of a necessity?

If a player exposes any or all of his own cards he can either play on with the exposed cards or pass them.

Many card rooms in the UK have a rule, which says, 'thinking time is restricted to two minutes'. This rule is open to interpretation and misinterpretation and is inconsistently applied. For an illustration of how the rule was applied in one very special circumstance see under the **Luck** heading in the Analysis of Hands chapter.

Etiquette

Courtesy should be paramount at the table but unfortunately it is sometimes lacking. Indeed, there are many examples of bad conduct witnessed at the poker table. Here are a few tips on how to conduct yourself with courtesy in the game. Try to remember that when your conduct is above reproach players will respect your opinion and will seek your guidance when there is a dispute.

- Do not pass your cards out of turn, even if you are no longer interested in staying in contest for the pot. It can affect the fortunes of one player over another when the field is shortened and a player has a difficult decision to make. It usually gives an advantage to the players seated before you who have yet to make their plays. You may see other players fold or call out of turn, but please don't do it yourself. If you do, be assured you will be pulled up by the other players for it.

- When discarding your hand do so at a low level of flight so that no other player can see what you have discarded.
- Leave your cards in plain view at all times, preferably on the table in front of you. Holding them against your shirt or showing them to 'railbird' friends (see Glossary) is not approved behaviour.
- Likewise, keep your chips in plain view at all times.
- Refrain from criticising other players' methods and standard of play.
- Do not abuse the dealer, verbally or in any other way. Bad behaviour, such as throwing cards at the dealer, whilst mercifully rare, is totally unforgivable. Remember it is not the dealer's fault that you are losing.
- Forget post-mortems. It is irritating for other players to have to listen to discussion on what happened in the last hand or even several hands ago.
- If you are plagued by the need to show someone what a good hand you had, when not required to do so at a showdown, make sure all players enjoy the same experience. The correct guideline often quoted at the poker table is 'show one, show all'.
- Showing your cards except at the showdown, even without bad intent, is bad etiquette.
- Players must not show or reveal the contents of their hands when all-in before betting is over. A player who shows that he has a strong hand for the centre pot hinders the chance of a player who bets into a side pot. There is less likelihood of a

call. If an all-in player shows that he has a weak hand he increases the chance of a call.

- Likewise, please don't feel that you have to tell everyone what your last hand was and what you would have had if only you had stayed in the pot, some polite people might feign interest, but few really are.
- Do not splash the pot. This is where a player throws his chips into the pot when making a bet. It takes extra time for the dealer to re-stack and count bets when you splash the pot. When you bet, place your chips directly in front of you. The dealer will then be sure you have bet the right amount and when betting is complete will place them into the pot.
- Soft-play agreements have a negative effect on the game. This is where a player bets less than they normally would or checks good hands when against friends, husbands or wives. Don't enter into these types of agreements. Every player should play in his own self-interest – it's the essence of poker.
- Do not handle other players' chips or cards.
- Speech play (also called 'coffee housing') is the term used to describe what happens when a player makes comments about a hand when it is in progress. This is not prohibited in terms of the rules, but it is considered unethical in the UK (not so in the USA). So be careful what you say during the play of a hand and resist the urge to talk about a hand during the action or when someone is thinking.
- Do not try to educate other players at the table by pointing out what you think are mistakes. Its odds on they will resent it and mark you down as a smart Alec, or worse. Why not let people pay for their education – it's how I had to learn!
- Players should speak up and assist the dealer by calling attention to an error in the amount of the bet or the improper reading of the hand etc. Likewise, any player who sees an error about to be made, such as awarding the pot to the wrong person, has a duty to speak up.

- It is improper to make an effort to see another player's hole card. However, one is not obliged to look away if any cards are openly exposed.
- Talk or actions demeaning to any person at the table are poor etiquette and should not be tolerated by the other players.
- A player going all-in should announce the fact and the dealer should make sure all players are aware of this circumstance.
- There are occasions when intent has to be considered when making decisions and observing the strict letter of the rule can be wrong. Therefore, one has to look behind the rule and look at the intent. Any signal to act, whether it be a tap on the table to signify check or other hand signal or verbal to signify raise, should be accepted by the players if it is understood by all what the player's intent was.
- Any player or person in authority has the right to inspect a deck of cards and change it at any time to protect the honesty and integrity of the game.
- When there are two players contending the pot to a showdown, both players may, if they wish, lay their cards down face up. If either player fails to do so any player can request all cards to be shown. However, the dealer must muck the cards that are being given up before exposure, i.e. touch the muck with the cards and then turn them over.

Actions by Players Considered Improper

It has to be remembered that poker is a game of deception. The following are a selection of reasons why certain actions, perhaps considered improper by some players, are not in fact bad etiquette.

- Players taking too long to act with a cinch hand may not be acting improperly as some forms of poker make it difficult to know the best hand before the showdown.

- Often, poor players do not know they have the nuts, therefore you should make allowances for them if they seem to take a long time to decide.
- It may be considered discourteous to slow play the nuts but it is not prohibited and some, including myself, would argue that it is not even bad etiquette. It is just one of the artifices of the game. Remember other players do not have to call.

Poker Practice

Never play cards with a man named 'Doc'.
Nelson Algren

Before you think about sitting down at a poker table there are several fundamental things that you should keep in mind. If you forget them you will be at a disadvantage before you start. For the sake of helping you to remember let's call these tips the guide to poker practice.

Alcohol Alcohol does not help you play better; it only makes you enjoy losing (that is until you wake up in the morning). So, your first guiding principle should be: Don't drink and play.

Bankroll Poker players call the money they use to play poker with their 'bankroll'. There is a saying in poker circles 'don't play with scared money' – that is, don't play with money you cannot afford to lose. If you do you are liable to play 'scared' and not give of your best. Believe me on this one, it is very difficult to call a bet when you know that if you lose you won't eat next week. This leads us to guiding principle number two: Play poker, particularly cash poker, only with money you can afford to lose.

Borrowing Money This is related to the point on bankroll. If you lose all of your playing cash don't borrow from other players. Remember that there will always be another game tomorrow and you don't have to reach into your pocket for more money, or worse still borrow from friends. If you do start on this route you will soon run out of friends. It is not often I get a chance to quote Shakespeare, but this one is from *Hamlet*: 'Neither a borrower nor a lender be; for loan oft loses both itself and friend, and borrowing dulls the edge of husbandry. This above all to thine own self be true.'

Control It is important to have the discipline to be able to get up from the poker table if things are going badly and just go home a loser. If you are playing in poker tournaments do so with the intention of limiting the number of re-buys you have and exercise control. Thus, the fourth guiding principle is to have control of your emotions. Not many players are good at controlling their self-destructive urges – if you can, you will immediately have an edge over your rivals at the poker table.

Cheating Deceit is an integral part of playing poker. In many ways it's what makes the game interesting, but it can spill over into cheating. Games run in European and US casinos are well managed and as a result cheating is rare at the poker table, but it does happen. Therefore, be wary, especially in home games. One form of cheating which is very difficult for the casinos to spot and hence to control is collusion between two or more players. This is where players are playing out of the same bankroll and may be communicating with each other via signals. So be vigilant.

Dos and Don'ts Do bet weak hands at high-stakes poker if you think there is a good chance you will not be called, but don't call with the same strength of hand. By betting in the first place your opponent indicates he has a strong hand. Another similar rule of thumb is don't call a bet unless you would call a raise.

Guard Your Hand I mention this one in the section on rules. Occasionally, a dealer will think a hand has been passed, because the player has seemed to push it away. These hands will be scooped up and put in with the other discards and the cards cannot be retrieved. It is each player's responsibility to guard his own cards. This can be done by being alert and/or putting a chip on top of live hands. Take care though that this behaviour does not produce any tells (see chapter on Reading Your Opponent)

Home Games You can leave casino games whenever you feel like it – you are under no obligation to play on, even if you are a big winner. Remember if it had been the other way round and you had lost all of your money you would have had to leave. However, some home games have rules (often not overtly stated) requiring winners to play on for a specified time. Usually, a winner will declare that he is going home in an hour's time or whatever. This is no bad thing in home games as most do not have a lot of players and games can break up if a few winners leave. In any case, if someone comes into a home game, plays a few hands, wins a big pot and then leaves ten minutes later, believe me that person will not be popular. Do it two weeks in a row and you will never be invited back.

Lending Money This is the next worst thing to borrowing money. By all means make up your own mind about it, but remember the odds are poor for getting paid back. Even when you do get the money back it can lead to undesired results. I once loaned someone £50 and sure enough I got it back, but a few days later I was asked for a loan of it again. It was repaid again, but asked for again, and so it went on until eventually I did not know who owned the £50 – me or the person who had borrowed it and seemed to have it more often than I did. In fact, eventually the person was asking me for the loan of *his* £50. So a good rule is: Don't lend money, it is an even quicker way to lose friends than borrowing money!

Mistakes The winner in the long term is the player who makes least mistakes. So when luck is against you, stay calm and play your normal game. If you lose your cool you will start to play badly and make more mistakes.

Novices You should never bluff a novice – they don't know the true strength of their own hand and are too likely to call.

Over the Top No, it is not being totally outrageous – in poker parlance it means re-raising an original raise. In particular, it usually refers to re-raising someone you think is bluffing. So if you think someone is 'on the steal' (bluffing), and you and this opponent have both got lots of chips, why not try going over the top. Beware though – it is best done against only one opponent, if there is a third party that person may have a legitimate hand.

Power Play Power play is a term used to describe playing hands in an aggressive way. There are different styles of aggression and different times when it is appropriate to be aggressive. Some players like to play aggressively with hands like A-A, K-K and A-K – that is, raise and re-raise by the amount of the pot or more if it is no-limit play. Other players will raise to reduce the field at a loose table before the flop, as the value of one's hand goes down the more callers there are, but they will take the risk and not re-raise hoping that they will get a caller after the flop. This second tactic is more risky. In most cases, it is probably best to use power play and re-raise. Some players don't like to be pushed around and will always come 'over the top' and re-raise with these hands. An aggressive style of play is most generally considered to be the winning way. But it is not the only way so don't be a slave to dogma and try to develop your own style.

Rocks A rock is the type of player who only enters a pot with the very highest grade of hand. You can easily spot rocks because they tend to sit a long time without playing a hand. An average player might play one in three hands, whereas a rock will play one in ten. Be very wary if this type of player enters the pot with you and be even more wary if the rock says something like 'let's gamble'. What the rock means is for you to gamble because be assured in this case that the rock will have a premium hand. By the way, a 'rock garden' is where there is a whole table of rocks. My best advice here is if you see a rock garden, make a run for the door!

Selection of Hands It's the cards you don't play that make you a winner – you must know when to throw them away.

Slow Playing This is where you bet a small amount with a strong hand in order to get more players into the pot and to deceive them as to the strength of your hand. It is often a bad strategy unless you have a blockbuster of a hand. Therefore, always make your opponent 'fold' or 'pay to play', never give a free card. It is often said that you can slow play a nut flush but not a nut straight.

Tight Play This means playing conservatively and only getting involved with strong hands. It is generally the right strategy, but a better piece of advice is to play tight at a loose table and loose at a tight table. A loose player plays too many hands, perhaps as many as eight in every ten. The advantage of playing tight at a loose table is fairly obvious, it means you can exploit the other players' weaker than average holdings. But what about playing loose in a tight game? Well in a tight game there is more opportunity to bluff and play with a bit of creativity and flair.

Weak Players There is a well-known saying in poker circles, 'If you look round the table and have not spotted a mug within twenty minutes, then it has to be you.'

Reading Your Opponent

Winning isn't everything. It is the only thing.
Vince Lombardi
(Coach of the superbowl winners, Green Bay Packers).

Poker is a complex and multifaceted game whose central facets are sometimes called the three Ps: patience, position (with regard to your proximity to the dealer) and psychology. In this chapter, I will focus on the last of these Ps which focuses on how to read the behaviour of your opponent: the psychology of poker.

Zia Mahmood, the world-class bridge player, is quoted as saying, 'One of the reasons I love the game of bridge is that there are no absolutely right answers to anything. Bridge is not a game that can be played mechanically, according to a series of rules. You have to use not only your brain and your memory but your imagination and your creative spark to avoid the traps that lie in even the simplest position.' The same description could just as easily be applied to the game of poker and the ability to analyse the behaviour of your fellow players is one of the subtlest and most difficult aspects of the game to master. In order to improve your game, it is important that you are able to observe closely how players behave and understand what, in percentage terms, these behaviours are likely to mean. Let's start with a few very simple examples – how players stack and handle their chips.

Chips

All casino games and some home games are played using 'chips' instead of money. In these situations the player would exchange his money for the same value of chips. There are a number of reasons for this, of which I will just give you two. Chips are easier to handle and count than money. Players can see at a glance whether an opponent has got a few or a lot of chips in front of them, whereas with a bundle of notes it is often impossible to know how much someone has. There is also a deeper psychological reason, seldom fully articulated, why casinos prefer players to use chips rather than money. When you exchange your money for chips, you have literally and figuratively exchanged something of real value for a playing token, for something that is once removed from money. I have seen people bet considerable sums at roulette and at the poker table using chips and, although it is a moot point, I sometimes wonder whether they would be so keen to make the same bet if they had to use the same fold-up money they used to pay for their groceries. There is a well known saying heard often in casinos and card rooms, that the person who invented casinos made a lot of money, but the person who invented chips made even more money.

Later on, we will examine the importance of 'stack' size – the number of chips that a person has stacked in front of him. A big stack will, depending on the monetary value or denomination of the chips, generally be more valuable than a short or medium stack. The size of stack you are playing and the size of the stack held by your opponents, are major factors to be considered when making a decision at the poker table.

Chip Handling

Some players divide their chips into separate piles, each pile having chips of the same value, others make one or two very tall piles with the bigger denomination chips at the bottom while others try to build structures resembling the Great Wall of China. Players will also differ in terms of how they put chips into the pot and what denomination of chips they use in different betting situations. Mostly these behaviours do not have any meaning that are discernibly useful, but below are a few examples of chip handling behaviours which I contend either offer an insight into a player's personality or give an indication of the value of the hand they are holding.

Example 1: Breaking the big note!

You may recall when you were younger, back in the days when to have a £5 note (or a $20 dollar bill for our American readers) was to be wealthy. In those days, if you had a big note, you did not like to 'break it' because once broken it tended to be spent much more quickly. The big note was something to be kept and prized. Some players treat their chips in this way. They are always wanting to give change, e.g. give you ten 100-unit chips for your 1000-unit chip and once they get the 1000-unit chip they like to hold on to it. (In contrast there are many players who are delighted to change big chips because a pile of small value chips looks more – see Example 4.) Watch this type of player closely because often, when they have a choice of putting small or large denomination chips into a pot, the choice of chips can have a meaning.

They will often put their small denomination chips into the pot when they have a marginal or perhaps a drawing hand. Sub-consciously, they may consider that they are not breaking into their pile of valuable chips, so they can do no real damage and can afford to speculate on this occasion. To continue the analogy with the 'big note', in this case they are only spending their small change. When this same player ignores his low denomination chips and puts in large value chips, then beware – there is a very high percentage chance that the player has a strong hand. Their subconscious reasoning may be that 'I will be getting these chips back anyway when I win the pot, therefore I don't need to put in small value chips. Also by putting in the high value chips the pot will be easier to count and the hand will be speeded up. I will get my reward sooner.'

Example 2: Little piles, little blinds

When the blinds for a tournament have reached, for example, the 600-unit stage, you will often observe a player building his chips into piles of exactly 600 units to make it easier to call the first bet. Then later when the blinds go up to 800 units this player will change the piles into stacks of 800-units value. This tells you something about the player. They are likely to be the type that calls much more often than they should, that is, in poker terminology, to be a 'calling station'. You cannot chase them out of the pot no matter how high your bet. It is best not to try stealing a pot or bluffing this type of player because the percentage chance is very high that you will be called. Conversely, if you have a reasonable hand you can try a bet because they are likely to call with a lesser hand.

Example 3: Don't hide your chips

Often at the poker table you will hear the cry 'Don't hide your chips.' This refers to the practice that some players have of hiding their high denomination chips behind several piles of smaller denomination chips. The explanation for this is often that the players hiding the chips are, both figuratively and actually, protecting their chips. This type of player tends to be 'tight' (that is, plays only very high value hands). So, if this type of player is in a pot with you be very careful. The percentage chance is high that the player will have a good hand.

Example 4: Big jar, small jars

As opposed to the type of player described in Example 1 who like to have small piles of high denomination chips, there are others who like to have big piles of small denomination chips. If the card room supervisor wants to change their small chips 'up' for those of bigger denomination, they want to keep the small value chips, 'because it looks more'. They seem to think that large piles of chips are more intimidating and, to some extent, I agree.

The French psychologist, Piaget, did a series of experiments with young children where he asked them to compare the quantities of liquids in glass jars of various sizes. In one version of the experiment, two of the glass jars were tall and each contained the same fixed quantity of liquid. There were also two smaller glass jars into which Piaget poured the contents of one of the larger jars. Piaget asked the children whether the tall jar, which remained full, contained the same quantity of liquid as the two smaller jars. His findings were that, in the early stages of development, children considered it natural for the quantity of the liquid to vary with the shape and dimensions of the containers into which it was poured. In other words, they did not have a fully developed concept of the conservation of matter or quantity.

Piaget was interested in the developing thought processes of children, so it would be rash to compare the cognitive processing of supposedly sophisticated poker players to that of small children. Still, it is possible that there may be perceptual processes which might make players perceive tall stacks as containing more chips than several smaller stacks.

A tall stack of chips in front of a player does seem to look more daunting than several small stacks, even though the total value might be the same in both cases. This is particularly so if a player has the small stacks one behind the other. There is no real empirical evidence for this observation but it often seems that players tend to be less inclined to bet into an opponent with a tall intimidating stack or stacks of chips in front of him than they would be to bet into anyone who has stacked the chips into several small piles. Although this is tentative advice, I do think there is merit in stacking your chips high.

Example 5: Macho man

I have never observed this behaviour in women players hence the title. Sometimes a man, usually an inexperienced player, will call a bet, or more often a raise, in such a way that there will be a cracking or snapping made by the chips as he bangs them into the pot. This usually happens after he pauses for thought. This behaviour is almost always a sign that he has a medium-strength hand. If it happens before the flop, in a raised Hold 'Em pot, this behaviour could indicate a fair hand such as K♦ Q♠ or A♣ 10♠ or even 7♦ 7♣ . Or, if it happens after a flop of say K♠ 6♥ 3♥ , it again would indicate a fair hand, perhaps K♣ 9♠ or K♣ 8♠ . This behaviour seems to me to be a non-verbal statement meaning 'I have a good hand and I am going to make a stand' (usually the player is mistaken in thinking he has a good hand). The player is also making a statement along the lines of 'you are not going to get away with a bluff against me'.

If in the former situation you are the one who raised with a proper raising hand, such as Q♠ Q♥ , then you have a big advantage because you are better able to put your opponent on a probable hand. If a higher card than your pair comes, you are in a much better position to gauge from his reaction whether it 'hits' one of his hole cards or not. Equally, in the latter case, if you hold say A♥ K♦ (when the flop was K-6-3), then you can bet with impunity.

A characteristic of this macho-type of player is often that they do not like to be check-raised. They tend to take it as an insult or perhaps even as an affront to their manhood, and they almost always call if they have a medium-strength hand. In our opinion this is one of the few situations where it is advantageous to check-raise in a pot-limit or no-limit game.

A word of caution

The very fact of committing the above observations to print may in itself change the behaviour of players and indeed, for purposes of deception, sophisticated players will often try to mimic the behaviours of less sophisticated players. Sometimes, for instance, your esteemed authors would make a bet purposely using small denomination chips when holding very strong hands. This is done just on the off-chance that a more sophisticated player will erroneously make the sort of deductions which we gave in Example 1. If no one makes this sort of a deduction – well, you have lost nothing by trying.

On the whole, the above chip-handling behaviours are only applicable to less sophisticated players. However, this is not always the case and sometimes you will see established players making fundamental errors. By revealing these chip-handling behaviours, I have, in a way, 'broken the magician's code' and told you how the card-reading trick is done. However, these are only a small sample of the range of chip-handling behaviours you will observe at the poker table. The challenge, for us all, is to interpret the behaviours and build up a repertoire of new card-reading tricks or analytical techniques.

Card-Handling Behaviours

Again you should be very attentive to how and when your opponents pick up and look at their cards. On the very simplest level, players are so careless sometimes that they pick up their cards in such a way that their neighbours cannot help but see what they are holding. These players are usually so poor that it is easy to determine what they are holding anyway, so I normally tell them to hide their cards.

Sometimes, players pick up their cards and look at them as soon as they get them, whilst others pick them up just before it is their turn to act. Just one example will be sufficient to let you know how careful observation and deduction can be used in 'reading' or determining what cards a player holds.

Example: Have I got a heart or not?

Often the flop in Hold 'Em will contain three cards all of the same suit, say [K♥] [7♥] [4♥]. When this happens one or more players may look at their hands again. The reason for this is that the player may have one card of the suit and has looked for the second time to make sure (see also Mike Caro's *Book of Tells* which is listed in the Bibliography). It is equally likely that the player has an ace but has forgotten what suit it is. In the case above, if the player has something like [A♥] [4♠] then this is a reasonable hand, but if he has [A♥] [K♠] then this is a more powerful hand. In both cases, if you have a flush already made and bet into the player they will more often than not call you. Some rash players even consider these 'drawing' hands to be good enough to bet, raise or re-raise with.

It is possible that a player will have something like [A♠] [K♣] against the [K♥] [7♥] [4♥] flop, in which case he should proceed with extreme caution because if this hand is out against a made flush there is practically no chance of the hand improving to win.

By watching what the player does in this sort of circumstance (i.e. the three-flush flop) you can obtain a very good impression of what cards he holds and play your own hand better as a result. So, for instance, if you are the player holding the [A♠] [K♣] against the [K♥] [7♥] [4♥] flop, you might well be prepared to proceed with the hand if you see your sole opponent have a second look at his cards. In this case, the chances are high that your opponent has a four-flush and that you are a percentage favourite in the pot (you would have an approximate 65 per cent chance of winning).

Incidentally, it is almost never the case that a player will pick up and look at their cards a second time if they already have the flush made. This is because if a player has two cards of the same suit he will remember what the suit is and even novice players will realise that it is giving the game away to look at their hand. This is why if you do have the flush on the flop and you are playing against sophisticated players it is sometimes deceptive to look at your cards a second time, pretending that you have only got four cards to the flush.

Chip and Card Behaviours

One brief example will illustrate how chip- and card-handling behaviours can combine to give you clues about what a player holds.

Example: I've got to protect my hand here!

Many players protect their hands from the danger of the dealer accidentally throwing it into the discards by the simple expedient of placing a chip or coin on top of the two-hole cards. Indeed some players even have special (perhaps 'lucky') chips which they use solely for this purpose. If such a player 'forgets' to put the chip on top of his cards it could be because the cards are not worth protecting. In general, when this happens the player is going to pass the cards in any case, so there is not much useful information to be drawn from this sort of observation.

Sometimes novices or poor players who don't have this habit of putting a chip on top of their cards will suddenly do so. You might even see the player take a whole stack of chips and pile them on top of his cards. When this happens, the player has almost invariably got a very good hand indeed (my money would be on two aces or two kings). Players in this circumstance may subconsciously get a feeling of paranoia that the dealer will rob them of a wonderful money-making opportunity by carelessly throwing their hand into the discards. Indeed there may be a different explanation for different players exhibiting this behaviour, but the important thing to bear in mind is that it does happen and reasonably frequently. If you observe a poor player piling chips onto his cards my advice is to pass unless you have the nuts.

However, as has been stressed at many points in this book, poker is a complex game and many players show feral cunning in the moves they make. So you should not take anything at face value. For instance, relatively sophisticated players who know about this type of card-protection behaviour may well stack chips on top of a worthless hand and then try to bluff you out of the pot.

More likely though is that a sophisticated player (let's call her Player X) will attempt to set someone up in the hope of winning a big pot. Player X will pick another intelligent player as her quarry and, knowing that this player is observant, will always pile chips on top of her good hands. Player X will make a point of ensuring that the quarry/victim sees the good hand on completion on each occasion. This type of behaviour will be reinforced by constant repetition (perhaps even over a period of a few nights), until Player X considers that her victim has the strongly held belief that 'Player X always piles chips on her good hands'. Then remarkably, when the two are in a big pot together, Player X will neglect to pile chips on her blockbuster hand and as a result will win a lot of extra chips from her hapless victim. Of course, this sort of trick should only work once against a good player.

This is only one example of how good players can set other players up for a 'coup de grâce' (or perhaps it could be called a 'coup de théâtre', because of the dramatic effect). So I would urge you to look out for this type of situation yourself.

Why does Player X pick another intelligent player as the victim? Why not a poor player? The reason is clear. It is because subtle play is lost upon poor players. They either don't notice or, if they do, it goes right over their heads. It seems like a paradox but you cannot do anything tricky against poor players and you should think carefully before trying to bluff a poor player. We are not saying don't try to bluff a poor player, just bear in mind that bluffs work best against intelligent players.

Above: Patrick Marber (left) and Stephen Fry (right) evaluate their hands on *Late Night Poker*'s Celebrity Challenge.

Below: The celebrity line-up of *Late Night Poker*'s Celebrity Challenge (left to right): Patrick Marber, Al Alvarez, Ricky Gervais, Stephen Fry, Antony Holden, Victoria Coren and Martin Amis.

Above: (left to right) Marina Rado, Nick Seremeta, Somkhuan Harwood, Thomas Kremser, Malcolm Harwood, Jesse May and Peter Schmid. Marina and Peter exhibit the highest standards in dealing and are known as the best on the European circuit.

Below: Shown here with fellow player Victoria Coren (right), Badar Islam (left), who also likes to be known as 'Big Big Badar' or 'Triple-B', is a renowned risk-taker at the poker table.

Right: Both familiar faces on the poker circuit, it is the ambition of Somkhuan Harwood (right) to beat husband Malcolm (left) head-to-head in a major tournament.

Above: Writer of the *Observer*'s poker column, Victoria Coren learned her poker skills from watching her brother and his friends as a teenager and has been hooked ever since.

Below: An aggressive, risk-taking player, Peter 'the bandit' Evans started his business with his winnings from the poker table.

Analysis of Hands

He who hesitates is last.
Mae West

There were many interesting hands that took place during the first two series of *Late Night Poker*, but it would not necessarily be instructive to analyse them all. In addition, such an analysis would be of limited use if it were not done as part of a larger analytical framework. Thus, I have picked out for analysis some key hands, mainly from the second series, which illustrate some common themes or commonly occurring situations. The themes I have chosen are:

1. Luck
2. Position
3. Aggressive play
4. Scaring off drawing hand
5. Semi-bluffs
6. Judgement calls
7. Slow playing
8. Common situations
9. Bluffs
10. Card-reading skills
11. Strong hand against strong hand

In addition, because it is the biggest festival of poker in the world, I have also used examples from the World Series of Poker where they illustrate one of the themes.

The World Series of Poker, held annually in Binion's Horseshoe Casino, Las Vegas, tends to bring together the very best players from all over the world. It is encouraging to see that many of the players who have appeared on *Late Night Poker* have also put up extremely good showings in World Series events. The third series of *Late Night Poker* will also see the first appearance of a past world champion, Phil Hellmuth. We are therefore analysing one of Phil's World Series hands.

1. Luck

Hand 1

This is from the semi-final of the second series and illustrates the fact that, despite excellent play, luck can often be a factor. This is a hand between Jonas Slovenia and Ross Boatman. Jonas is the host of a Slovenian chat show and Ross Boatman is a London-based actor well known for his role in *London's Burning*. Ross is following in the footsteps of some other (perhaps more famous) actors like the late Telly 'Kojak' Savalas and Gabe Kaplan by being an extremely accomplished poker player. The hand developed as follows:

Jonas held [A♦] [K♦] and raised the bet to £300.

Ross re-raised all-in with [A♠] [K♠].

Jonas called.

The board came [Q♠] [7♠] [8♠] [9♥] [3♠].

Jonas went out having played the hand (of identical value to Ross's) perfectly well but having suffered bad luck.

The theme of luck cannot be emphasised too much as it is a factor in all poker games. Over the long term, each individual player gets as much good luck as bad. Hence skill comes into play in that good players will minimise their losses during a run of bad luck but maximise their gains during a good run (or a 'rush' as some players would call it).

Hand 2

This hand illustrates one of the most famous recent pieces of poker bad luck. In addition, it illustrates the sort of 'at the table' analysis that sophisticated players are able to make. It is the final hand in the main event of the World Series of Poker 2000. This tournament takes four days to play and is the ultimate test of a poker player's stamina and character.

When the tournament got down to the last two players, T J Cloutier was up against Chris (Jesus) Ferguson, not an unknown in Vegas poker circles, but certainly less famous than his opponent. However, to compensate for this, he had 90 per cent of the chips.

Cloutier soon got to work. A master at head-up play, he had Ferguson on the run. Time after time, he would bet or raise and Ferguson would throw his hand away. Soon, Cloutier was nearly level. Then came the key hand. Ferguson made an initial small raise and Cloutier moved all-in. Ferguson thought for five minutes before calling. (That he was allowed such time might surprise some readers. As stated in the chapter on rules, many card rooms in the UK have a rule that 'thinking time is restricted to two minutes'. But two minutes from when? Most dealers don't wear watches. The correct rule is two minutes from when another player requests that a player be 'put on the clock'.) The dealer should have no authority to put a player on the clock. Thus, if Cloutier said nothing (as in this case), Ferguson could have sat there for half an hour if he'd wanted to. However, even five minutes can be a long time sitting at a poker table when nothing is happening.

He called. The hands were turned over. Cloutier had A-Q offsuit, Ferguson A-9 suited.

I must confess the first time I heard this I thought Ferguson had made a poor call but actually it was quite clever. Here's why.

I suspect that Ferguson realised that he was up against a superior player (this is something a lot of players would be reluctant to admit). So what does he think Cloutier has? Remember, Cloutier had moved all-in, a bet much bigger than the size of the pot, so he's unlikely to be bluffing.

1. **A Small Pair** This would be ideal for Ferguson, as he'd then be about even money to win the tournament. But would Cloutier go all in with, for example, two 4s?

2. **A Medium or Big Pair** This is much more likely. It wouldn't be a disaster, however, because Ferguson could still hit his ace and win (unless he is very unlucky and Cloutier has two aces). He'd be about two to one against if facing any pair but aces.

3. **Ace-High Kicker** A-K, A-Q or A-J. This seems to be most likely. Again Ferguson's not out of it, though, because he could still hit his 9 and win. Here, he'd be about five to two against.

4. **Two High Cards** K-Q or K-J. This seems most unlikely. Cloutier would be more inclined to just call with such a hand. Ferguson would be slight favourite here, though.

Ferguson probably took the view that he could take a stand with his A-9 where he was likely to be at worst, five to two against, or he could keep on folding and let Cloutier 'ante' him away. On balance, it wasn't such a bad decision.

What happened? The flop came K-4-2. Fourth street was another king. So, on the river, Ferguson needed a 4 or a 2 to tie. But a 9 would win him the tournament and the title of world champion. And a 9 is what came. Ferguson was crowned as champion and received the $1,500,000 first prize whilst Cloutier, who was most gracious in defeat offering the winner his warm congratulations, received a mere $896,500. Nevertheless, Cloutier's bad luck cost him some $600,000 or £400,000.

2. Position

From heat three of the second series, this hand illustrates the importance of having good position over an opponent and is also an example of a successful bluff. This is a hand between Bill Shervington and Barney Boatman. Bill is a chess player and, perhaps more unlikely, he is part of the hunting, shooting and fishing fraternity. He likes to apply his field-sport insights at the poker table. Barney is the older brother of Ross (see previously under **Luck**) and has had a variety of occupations over the years, including painting and decorating and computer programming. He now plays poker for a living and is just as formidable as his brother at the table. Most of Barney's acting skills have been honed at the poker table. It is a toss-up as to which of the Boatman brothers is the better player. I certainly would not like to choose between them.

Bill with A-10 raises £50.

Barney calls with A-Q.

The flop came: Q-6-3.

Barney, who was first to act, bet £175.

Bill re-raises.

Barney calls but seems reluctant about it, with a flop like this he has to suspect that he is walking into trips. Bill may have interpreted Barney's reluctant call as an indication of weakness which, with better position, he can later take advantage of.

Fourth street brings a K.

Barney checks.

Bill bets. Here he exploits his better position and also makes a fine successful bluff.

Barney folds the best hand, which was a cautious play but sometimes it pays to be cautious in poker and at least he lives to fight another day. Also, remember that a good rule of thumb in poker is that you can only bluff good players.

3. Aggressive play

Hand 1

This hand is from heat three of the second series and is between Dave Welch and Chip Winton. Dave Welch has been playing poker for over ten years and spends some 60 per cent of his time playing these days; the remainder of the time he devotes to running his transport business. Chip Winton, from Texas, is a senior executive with an express delivery business in the USA. He plays poker as a hobby, but brings a lot of his business acumen to the table. This hand illustrates the importance of aggressive play.

The flop came: J-4-3.

Dave bets £75 with J-5 (top pair with a very poor kicker).

Chip raises with a J-10 (top pair with a moderately poor kicker). Dave calls.

Fourth street pairs the board with another 4.

Dave checks.

Chip bets £75, which is a small bet for size of pot – this possibly shows weakness which Dave exploits with aggressive play.

Dave raises to £475. This is a check-raise which in this situation is a very aggressive play that wins the pot as Chip passes the best hand. In this case Dave had bad position but overcame it by adopting an aggressive check-raise strategy.

Hand 2

This hand is taken from the final of the first series of *Late Night Poker* and illustrates the benefits to be derived from aggressive play. When the action got down to five-handed, a big hand developed between Surinder Sunar, Peter (the Bandit) Evans and Dave (Devilfish) Ulliot. Surinder is a Birmingham-based professional player who developed an interest in poker while at university. Subsequently, he started playing in small tournaments and now plays in the biggest games he can find. He has been in all of the *Late Night Poker* series so far and is becoming well known for his daring play. Peter is one of poker's gentleman players, who now runs his own business, which he started with his poker winnings.

Peter made it £2,000 to go, which is a typically aggressive play by the Bandit, hoping for a steal. Devilfish flat called, but Surinder, not to be out-matched in terms of aggression, made a big re-raise of £6,000, enough to almost put the Bandit all-in.

Here's what the hands were:

Surinder	Bandit	Devilfish
K-J Offsuit	9♦ 7♦	A-Q Offsuit

Surinder must have taken the view that when Devilfish only flat called, he didn't have a big hand. Thus his very aggressive re-raise was designed to win the pot there and then, or push the Devilfish out and get head up with the Bandit. That's what happened, as the Bandit went all-in. Devilfish passed his ace-queen which was, ironically, the best hand of the three.

The board cards were 10♠ 9♣ 8♥ 7♠ 7♥.

Surinder made a straight on fourth street, but the Bandit filled a full house on the river. This left Surinder with a severe dent in his stack and to use a poker expression 'talking to himself' as the Bandit became the new leader. In this example, both of the players who made aggressive plays managed to make the person holding the best hand before the flop pass. However, although Devilfish, generally considered a very aggressive player himself, passed on this occasion he eventually went on to win the first series. Sometimes it is perhaps better to temper aggression with some cool-headed discretion.

4. Scaring off drawing hand

From heat four of the second series, this is an example of not betting enough to scare off a drawing hand. The hand is between Lee Drebbin and Malcolm Harwood. Lee is from Blackpool and works as a housing project manager. He considers himself to be a recreational player. Malcolm, in contrast, has been playing for 42 years and is now a full-time professional poker player. He started playing in the RAF in 1958 when he was doing his national service and is one of the most friendly and gregarious players on the European circuit. The hand developed as follows:

Four players stay for a flop of [9♥] [8♥] [3♦].

Lee has 9-9 making top trips but he has to be wary of players staying with four-flushes and four-straights hoping to fill their hands. He bets £400 but perhaps should have bet more to discourage the draws.

Malcolm calls with [A♥] [6♥].

Fourth street brings the [10♥], making it possible that a flush or a straight is out.

Lee checks.

Malcolm bets £200.

Lee calls. He must suspect that he is behind but is hoping to fill the full house.

Fifth street brings the [7♥] (making a straight flush for Malcolm).

Malcolm bets £200 all-in.

Lee passes his trips as now there are four cards to the straight flush on the board. On the flop, Lee has a classic dilemma. Does he bet a large amount knowing that he will win the pot there and then but have no possibility of gaining more from an extremely good hand? Or, does he take the risk and let his opponent in cheap? Lee took the latter course and it did not pay off on this occasion. On other occasions, however, it might have worked well for him.

5. Semi-bluffs

From heat five of the second series, this is an example of a player making a semi-bluff raise with a drawing hand. The hand is between Blackpool-based player Howard Plant and Peter (the Bandit) Evans.

Howard and Peter both call a flop containing [K♠] [J♥] [10♠].

Peter has A-K and bets £400.

Howard has [Q♠] [4♠] and raises to £1000 (Howard has a very strong drawing hand, he is drawing to both flush and straight); this is a semi-bluff raise.

Peter re-raises, putting himself all-in, and Howard calls.

Fourth street brings a [K♣] giving Peter three kings and Howard still has his draw.

Fifth street is a [5♥] meaning that Peter wins and Howard's draw has been unsuccessful. Howard's hand was actually a slight favourite on the flop, but this example illustrates the fact that sometimes both players in a heads-up situation can play optimally and eventually the result is a matter of luck.

6. Judgement calls

From heat five of the second series, this hand again features Howard Plant. His opponent this time is Charalambos Xanthos, otherwise known as Bambos, a restaurant and hotel owner, now based in London. Bambos is very calm and methodical at the poker table; nothing seems to faze him. This is an example of Bambos making a judgement call.

Howard bets £300 with 9-8.

Bambos raises to £900 with A-Q and Howard calls.

The flop comes K-7-6.

The board is completed with no more betting to make K-7-6-J-J.

Neither player has any sort of a hand, but Howard tries a bluff with a bet of £900 (it's the only way that Howard can win the pot which by this time is worth a lot of money).

Bambos, however, calls with only an ace high to win the pot, thus making what in many people's opinion was the best judgement call in *Late Night Poker* to date. Indeed, this may be the best hand of the tournament and Bambos demonstrated excellent card- and player-reading skills.

7. Slow playing

From heat seven of the second series, this is an example of a player slow playing top trips. The hand is between Hamish Shah and Tom Gibson. Hamish is a stockbroker based in London. Although he's been playing regularly for ten years, he says he plays mostly as a pastime. Tom is from County Kildare, Ireland, and is a former civil servant who currently lives in Dublin. Tom has given up the civil service and now plays poker for a living.

In this pot, Hamish has A-A and raises the pot to £100, Tom calls with A-J.

The flop brings **A♣** **10♣** **7♥** and fourth street a **6♠** .

Tom bets £200 with his ace-good kicker and Hamish calls. Here Hamish is slow playing his monster hand (trip aces), but note he is taking a risk in potentially letting Tom draw for a flush or straight.

Fifth street brings a **K♠** .

Tom checks and Hamish bets £200. Tom calls and Hamish wins the pot.

8. Common situations

Hand 1

From heat seven of the second series, this hand is an example of a common situation which often occurs in tournament play. A small pair is up against two overcards which is effectively even money on both hands. The hand is between Marty Wilson and Somkhuan Harwood. Based in Wolverhampton, he says he got his nickname 'Mad Marty' because of the way he is – one day he is cash rich and the next day he's got nothing. Somkhuan has been playing for seven years but considers that she is still learning with every game she plays. Her advice to beginners is to get a good teacher. She feels that she has been lucky in this respect, learning a lot from her husband Malcolm (see previously under **Scaring off drawing hand**). Somkhuan's ambition in poker is to beat her husband head-to-head in a decent competition (she thinks he would 'go bananas').

Marty has A-K and, as he is short of chips, goes all-in for £500. Somkhuan calls with 3-3.

The board comes 10-10-10-6-4.

Somkhuan wins with a full house. For all practical purposes it was even money on both players for the hand, but Somkhuan's hand held up and Mad Marty has to count himself unlucky.

Hand 2

From the final of the second series, this is an example of where a player fills a hand by the 'backdoor'. The hand is between Debbie Berlin and Malcolm Harwood.

Here the flop brings J♥ 7♥ 6♥.

Debbie bets £500 with A♥ 10♠. This is a semi-bluff as Debbie has a four-flush and one over card. If another player has a jack (making two jacks) or better they are slight favourites over Debbie's hand.

This turns out to be the case as Malcolm holds 7-7 making trip sevens. Malcolm only calls. Note that this is not another example of slow playing a hand, for although Malcolm is taking the risk of letting Debbie complete her draw, he has to fear that she has made a flush already.

The other players in this pot all pass.

Fourth street brings a 8♦, which does not help Malcolm but means that Debbie is now drawing for both a flush and a straight.

Both players check, probably each fearful of what the other holds.

Fifth street brings a 9♦, making a straight for Debbie. This straight was completed by the backdoor, as it was made using both of the last two cards and Debbie was originally drawing to the flush.

Debbie bets £1000 and Malcolm wisely passes his trips.

9. Bluffs

Hand 1

From the final of the second series, this is an example of a successful bluff. The hand is between Ram Vaswani and Ross Boatman.

Ross has J-10 and raises the bet to £1,800.

Ram calls with K-J (Ram is not to know but he is a big favourite).

The flop is A-5-4.

Ross bets all-in, which is a pure bluff. Ross has nothing, but he is representing two aces – his bet indicates that a likely hand for him to hold is A-x, where x equals any kicker, but his pre-flop raise indicates a high kicker.

Ram passes thus Ross has been successful with his bluff.

Hand 2

This is an example of unsuccessful bluff and judgement call, again selected from the final of the second series. The hand is between Simon Trumper and Ram Vaswani.

Ram holds K-10 and Simon a worthless 5-3.

The flop brings 10-9-8.

Ram bets £1400 as he has top pair with a good kicker.

Simon raises £4000 more which is a pure bluff.

Ram calls and the next two cards are 9-Q.

Simon bets, continuing the bluff, but Ram calls and wins.

10. Card-reading skills

From the third heat of the second series, this is an example of good card-reading skills. The hand is between Simon Trumper and Bill Shervington. Simon is a semi-professional player who started in £10 games in Reading and has only been playing for some five years. Simon is the winner of the second series of *Late Night Poker* and considers it to be his best poker experience to date.

Bill has J-J and raises £75.

Simon calls with 6-5 (these small connecting cards can often be played if it is not too expensive to call).

The flop brings 9-6-5.

Bill bets with his overpair to the flop. Simon raises because he must know he is winning at this point due to Bill's pre-flop raise. The pre-flop raise allows Simon to 'put Bill on' or read him for a big pocket pair.

Bill now goes all-in possibly thinking that Simon holds something like A-9 (i.e. top pair top kicker).

Fourth street brings a 6, making a full house for Simon. The only card that can help Bill now is another jack. But the last card is a 7 and Simon wins.

11. Strong hand against strong hand

Hand 1

This hand is from the World Championship Final of the 1989 World Series of Poker, where the last two were Johnny Chan (winner in both 1988 and 1987) and 24-year-old new kid on the block Phil Hellmuth. If Hellmuth were to win, he would be the youngest winner thus far. If Chan won, he would equal Johnny Moss's record of three wins and be the first to win three times in a row. Now sadly no longer with us, Moss had dominated the tournament in its early years. He won in 1970 (when the players voted on the champion) and again in 1971 and 1974.

Hellmuth had about a two to one lead in chips when the final hand was played. First to speak, he made it $40,000 to go. Chan called and re-raised $130,000. Hellmuth then immediately said he was all-in. Chan now had a tough call. He had about half a million dollars left, as against Hellmuth's million or so with about $300,000 in the pot. But if Chan called and won, he'd be a solid favourite. The hands were:

Chan	Hellmuth
[A♠][7♠]	9-9

This is similar to the decision Chris Ferguson faced against T J Cloutier. He is probably behind, but will be no worse than about 5/2 against to win it. The difference here though is that Hellmuth has an aggressive image, so Chan could easily put him on a hand such as a K-Q, in which case Chan would be favourite. Nevertheless, I think it was a marginal call since Chan had not made such a huge commitment to the pot that he could not pass. But then he's got umpteen World Series Bracelets, which is umpteen more than me, so who am I to argue? Chan called. With a spade draw and an overcard, he's about 2/1 against.

The flop was [K♦][K♣][10♥] with fourth street the [Q♠]. Chan would now be saved if the river was a 10 (two pairs), jack (straight), queen (two pairs) or an ace. But Hellmuth was delighted to see the [6♠], and his two nines held up. So, on this occasion, the best hand on the flop won and there were no issues with bad luck as in the 2000 final. Phil Hellmuth became the youngest ever champion and since then has gone from strength to strength. He is now generally considered one of the strongest players in the world.

Hand 2

The first big hand of the final of the second series of *Late Night Poker* involved Debbie Berlin, Dave (Devilfish) Ulliot and Ram Vaswani. This hand illustrates several themes and shows what happens when a strong hand comes up against another strong hand.

Ram raised the pot to £700 before the flop with pocket sixes and was called on the button by Devilfish and on the big blind by Debbie. The hands were as follows:

Devilfish	Debbie	Ram
[K♥][J♥]	[K♣][10♥]	[6♠][6♣]

The flop was [K♦][6♥][3♥].

Debbie has a reasonable hand, hitting kings on the flop and she bet £500. Ram just called (he was slow playing his trips – a great hand), hoping to get some action behind him. Devilfish re-raised to £2500 with two kings and a flush draw with another very strong hand. Debbie folded but Ram re-raised again going all-in and Devilfish called. Devilfish has top pair with a good kicker plus four to the flush, but must suspect he is behind. However, there is now too much in the pot for him to pass and he knows he has lots of outs (this is an example of a two-way hand which we looked at in the Playing Your Hand chapter). The turn and river cards were a running pair of fours (4♦ followed by 4♥), making a flush for Devilfish but a winning full house to Ram.

Hand 3

Another hand from the final of the second series involved a similar type of confrontation with a strong hand matched against another strong hand. It is also an example of a semi-bluff that has gone wrong. Bambos and Simon Trumper were the players.

Simon, holding A♣ 8♣ raised on the button and Bambos called with K♠ Q♠.

The flop came A♦ 8♠ 7♠.

Simon bet out with the top two pair. Bambos raised all-in with a king-high flush draw. He cannot beat a pair, so his hope is to win the pot on the flop with this semi-bluff. It's hard to get someone holding the top two pair in Texas Hold 'Em to pass, so not surprisingly Simon calls. Fourth street brought the A♠, giving Bambos his flush but Simon a full house.

Hand 4

The undoubted key hand of the final of the first series, if not the whole series, involved Dave Welch who raised before the flop with pocket jacks and Dave (Devilfish) Ulliot. Devilfish called, slow playing his pocket aces.

The flop came A♠ 10♣ 5♥.

Devilfish checked his monster hand (i.e. trip aces). Dave Welch, with two jacks, cannot have liked the flop, but he bet, in an effort to win it right there. He knew that if he got called, he was probably up against an ace, perhaps with a weak kicker, and he would definitely slow down after that. Devilfish called again slow playing his trips. Because there is no likely draw on the flop, Devilfish was quite safe in not raising. Dave's raise before the flop indicated that he was not likely to have two small cards and hence a draw to a bottom straight.

Devilfish was trying to keep Dave Welch interested. If he had raised then, Dave would have undoubtedly passed. Fourth street was the eight of hearts, no visible improvement. Devilfish checked yet again and Welch wisely checked behind him. Dave Welch was hoping this hand was going to be checked out but he was out of luck. The river was the four of diamonds. The board now looked like this: A♠ 10♠ 5♥ 8♥ 4♦

Devilfish then bet enough to set Dave all-in. If he checked again here, he knew that Dave would probably just turn his hand over. So he had to bet. This was a tough call for Dave Welch. There was no likely draw that Devilish could have made, except for the remote possibility of the small straight, so it looked like he had an ace or was bluffing. I wouldn't have liked to choose. In fact, Dave Welch even said to Devilfish that he had either a very strong hand or was on a complete bluff, which was a good analysis. However, Dave called and Devilfish showed his aces. This defining hand allowed Dave (Devilfish) Ulliot to go on and eliminate Peter the Bandit and win the first title of *Late Night Poker* champion and collect the £40,000 prize money. Peter the Bandit finished a creditable second and collected £7,000.

Tournaments

A poker tournament or competition is an event where the players all contend for a cash prize. As in *Late Night Poker* and the World Series of Poker, both of which are tournaments, each player pays an initial buy-in and receives a fixed number of tournament chips. The competitors play until all but one are eliminated and the remaining player is the winner of the event. It is usual for the last three finishers in a tournament to receive a prize from the prize pool. The division of prizes in small tournaments is usually something like 60 per cent to the winner, 30 per cent to the second and 10 per cent to the third. In bigger tournaments, the first ten players might receive a prize, perhaps split 45 per cent to the winner, 20 per cent for second, 10 per cent for third, 5 per cent for fourth and so on until all of the prize money has been allocated.

Tournaments are of two types: those that allow re-buys and those that do not. The latter are called 'freeze-out tournaments'. *Late Night Poker* is an example of a freeze-out event and once a player has lost all his chips he is out of the tournament. Those tournaments which permit re-buys allow a player who has lost all of his chips to re-join the tournament by paying additional money into the prize pool. It is usual for re-buys to be limited to the first time period of the tournament (usually the first 1½–2 hours).

After the re-buy period has ended, the tournament then becomes a freeze-out and the size of the blinds (and hence the stakes) increase with time to speed the tournament's end. If the blinds did not increase in this way, tournaments would last for days

instead of the usual four to five hours. Often, the blinds increase
regularly every 20 or 30 minutes in a small tournament but it can
be slower in bigger events. Typical increases and intervals are:

Small Tournaments			Bigger Tournaments		
Time Interval	Small Blind	Big Blind	Time Interval	Small Blind	Big Blind
1st 90 mins	50	50	1st 2 hours	50	100
20 mins	100	100	next 1 hour	100	200
20 mins	200	200	next 1 hour	200	400
20 mins	400	400	next 1 hour	400	800
20 mins	600	600	next 1 hour	600	1200
20 mins	800	800	next 1 hour	800	1600
20 mins	1000	1000	next 1 hour	1000	2000
20 mins	2000	2000	next 1 hour	2000	4000
20 mins	3000	3000	next 1 hour	3000	6000

As the tournament progresses, tables are aggregated and seats
removed as players are eliminated. This will eventually produce a
final table of ten contestants who battle it out for the prize pool.

Satellites

Sometimes a tournament is too expensive for some players to
enter. The entry fee might be £6000 and beyond the pocket of most
players. In these cases, it is normal for satellite tournaments to be
held with the winner gaining entry to the tournament proper. In
this way, it is not unknown for players to invest as little as £50 and
end up with a prize of £20,000.

General Hints on Tournament Play

Poker tournaments provide an opportunity to win big prizes for small outlays, thus many players now prefer them to cash poker. However, the strategy required for tournament play is significantly different from that required in cash games. Tournaments work by eliminating players who lose all their chips. Your twin aims in tournament play are thus to amass chips but at the same time to do everything in your power to avoid being eliminated. In freeze-out tournaments, the latter aim is even more important because there is no opportunity for re-buys.

Mason Malmuth (See Bibliography.) states that in re-buy tournaments it is always mathematically correct to re-buy and that this rule holds even if all the other players at the table have many more chips than you will have after your re-buy. However, some other authorities advise against taking this policy too far.

One aspect of tournament play which differs from cash-game play is that competitors need to be very patient. This does not necessarily mean waiting patiently for a good hand but rather it means waiting for good opportunities. By opportunity here I mean a combination of good position, good read on your opponent and possibly a good hand as well. In cash games, you might be prepared to take a risk with, for instance, a drawing hand giving you a 33 per cent chance of winning the pot because you are getting good pot odds. This would be correct in cash games because you know that if you make the play in similar situations over a series of hands you will show a profit. The same reasoning does not apply in freeze-out tournaments or tournaments where the buy-in phase has ended. In a tournament, if you play a hand with 33 per cent chance of winning, no matter how good the pot odds, you are putting yourself in the position where you have a 66 per cent chance of being eliminated. If you lose in cash games, you can just take more money out of your pocket, but in a tournament, after the buy-ins are over, you do not have this option. So patience and caution are valuable assets in tournament play.

However, in the early stages of a re-buy tournament many players will take more risks than they would in a cash game, in the hope of building up a large stack of chips. This is not a bad policy during the re-buy stage, where you could play the 33 per cent draw, because the worst that can happen is that it will cost you another re-buy. Also, in the early stages of a tournament, the cost of the blinds will be low compared to the average number of chips held by the players, which allows looser play. This is not a bad policy provided you can afford to re-buy. If you cannot afford the re-buy you will have to play a lot more cautiously.

In the middle and later stages of a tournament, the structure of the game gradually changes. The blinds increase until eventually they become very large in comparison to the size of the average stack. Adopting tactics which allow you to win the blinds, therefore, becomes increasingly important and you will find that players bluff and semi-bluff much more. This is usually correct tactics. However, it now becomes less correct to just call bets speculatively mainly because it costs too much compared to the size of the stacks.

In the later stages of a tournament, stack size is all-important. A large stack is much to be feared because that player can eliminate you from the tournament. But you can more readily play against small stacks as they can do you no terminal damage, even if they win a few pots from you. If you are one of the lucky ones and have a big stack, you can take more risks and perhaps call a bit more than you would otherwise, particularly against the small stacks.

In the later stages of the tournament, players begin to be eliminated more quickly and often you will have to play at a table with between five and eight players (as opposed to the optimum nine to eleven). This means that you will have to put in a blind bet more often, for each round of the table, therefore costing you more to play than at a full table. You now need to win hands more frequently just to maintain the size of your stack. In these situations, it becomes correct to play more loosely, that is, to play more hands. The trick though is not just to play more hands, but to play them aggressively, hoping that your bets will win the pot for you uncontested.

Final Table Play

At the final table in small to medium-sized tournaments, there is usually a prize for the first three or four players, so you will have a 30–40 per cent chance of getting in the money. The temptation is to be very cautious. However, because the blinds are extremely high at this stage compared to the average stack and, also, because, as players are eliminated, the cost per round to play increases, it is seldom correct to play too cautiously. You will get anted away if you don't win at least one hand for every round of the table.

It has become common practice in tournaments throughout the world for the last few players in a tournament to do a deal sharing the prize money between them. A rough estimate is that this happens at least 50 per cent of the time. For instance, if the four remaining players all have roughly the same number of chips, it is not unusual for the players to split the prize money equally, with each getting 25 per cent. Another type of common deal is where the remaining players agree to take a fixed sum each and play for the rest of the prize money. So, if there was £5000 in prize money, the four players might agree to take £1000 each and play for the remaining £1000.

Where to Play

Getting married is serious business. It's kinda formal, like funerals or playing stud poker.
Robert Ardrey

United Kingdom and Ireland

There are some 120 casinos in the United Kingdom and about a third of them spread poker games of some sort. In addition, there are two card clubs in Dublin and a recently opened card club in Birmingham, the Elite Club.

Many people are somewhat overwhelmed on their first visit to a casino card room. They do not know what to expect and probably have the feeling that everyone there, except them, is an expert. However, take my advice, this impression is entirely wrong and there is nothing to be intimidated about. In UK card rooms, there is usually a member of casino staff on hand to help with enquiries and, despite the often forbidding facades, most card players are only too delighted to help beginners. (Could this be enlightened self-interest?)

Casino and card club addresses where poker is played, correct at the time of writing, are given below in alphabetical order of the town or city name. This is not necessarily an exhaustive list and venues and nights of play are constantly changing, so you should phone your local casino/s to find out what they have on offer.

A

Ladbroke Casino Club
59 Summer Street
Aberdeen
AB1 2SJ
Tel: 01224 645 273
Fax: 01224 643 730

B

The Rainbow Casino
1 Portland Road
Edgbaston
Birmingham
B16 4HN
Tel: 0121 454 1033
Fax: 0121 545 5967

The China Palace
16–18 Hurst Street
Birmingham
B5 4BN
Tel: 0121 622 3313
Fax: 0121 622 6528

Elite Sporting Club
450 Moseley Road
Moseley
Birmingham
B12 9AN
Tel : 0121 683 8899

Grosvenor Casino
Grand Hall Buildings
15 Station Road
Blackpool
FY4 1EU
Tel: 01253 406 898
Fax: 01253 342 732

Ladbroke Casino Club
48 Westover Road
Bournemouth
BH1 2BZ
Tel: 01202 553 790
Fax: 01202 315 116

Napoleon's Casino Club
37 Bolton Road
Bradford
BD1 4DR
Tel: 01274 391 820
Fax: 01274 725 467

Grosvenor Casino
88–92 Queens Road
Brighton
BN1 3XE
Tel: 01273 326 514
Fax: 01273 326 964

C

Ladbroke Casino Club
8–16 Park Chambers
Park Place
Cardiff
CF1 3DQ
Tel: 029 20 344 221
Fax: 029 20 344 221

Annabelle Casino (Stanley Leisure)
11–12 King William Street
Coventry
CV1 5NA
Tel: 024 76 223 256
Fax: 024 76 525 441

D

Stanley Derby Casino
2 Colyear Street
Derby
DE1 1LA
Tel: 01332 368 880
Fax: 01332 295 218

Ladbroke Hotel Casino
Central Promenade
Douglas
Isle of Man
IM2 4NA
Tel: 01624 662 662
Fax: 01624 625 535

Ladbroke Casino
Earl Grey Place
Dundee
DD1 4DE
Tel: 01382 201 888
Fax: 01382 223 208

Jackpot Club & Colossus Club
20 & 5A Montague Street
Dublin 2
Tel: +353 1 478 5858
The clubs are sited across the street from each other and have the same owners.

E

Stanley Berkeley Casino
2 Rutland Place
Edinburgh
EH2 2AD
Tel: 0131 228 4446
Fax: 0131 228 8735

Stanley Edinburgh Casino
5b York Place
Edinburgh
EH1 3EB
Tel: 0131 624 2121
Fax: 0131 557 4386

G

Grosvenor Casino
100 High Street
Gorleston-on-sea
Great Yarmouth
NR31 6RG
Tel: 01493 652 810
Fax: 01493 603 440

Ladbroke Rotunda Casino
28a Tunnel Street
Glasgow
G3 8HL
Tel: 0141 243 2430
Fax: 0141 243 2420

Ladbroke Riverboat Casino
61 Broomielaw
Glasgow
G1 4RJ
Tel: 0141 221 6000
Fax: 0141 221 9488

L

Grosvenor Casino
Moortown Corner House
Harrogate Road
Leeds
LS17 6LD
Tel: 0113 269 5051
Fax: 0113 269 6118

Grosvenor Casino
76–78 West Derby Road
Liverpool
L6 9BY
Tel: 0151 260 8199
Fax: 0151 263 3986

Grosvenor Victoria Casino
150–166 Edgware Road
London
W2 2DT
Tel: 020 7 262 7777
Fax: 020 7 724 1214

Ladbroke Russell Square Casino
The Imperial Hotel
61–66 Russell Square
London
W1CB 5BA
Tel: 020 7 833 1881
Fax: 020 7 833 1871

Grosvenor Casino
Dunstable House
50 Dunstable Road
Luton
LU1 1EE
Tel: 01582 414 166
Fax: 01582 24 057

M

Grosvenor Casino
2 Empire Street
Cheetham Hill
Manchester
M3 1JA
Tel: 0161 834 8433
Fax: 0161 832 7104

N

Stanley Casino
Forth Street
Newcastle upon Tyne
NE1 3NZ
Tel: 0191 232 0900
Fax: 0191 232 2197

Ladbroke Regency Casino
Regent Street
Northampton
NN1 2LA
Tel: 01604 24 916
Fax: 01604 34 908

R

Grosvenor Casino
The Pavilion
Harbour Parade
Ramsgate
CT11 8LS
Tel: 01843 585 678
Fax: 01843 581 383

Grosvenor Casino
Queens Road
Reading
RG1 4SY
Tel: 0118 959 4642
Fax: 0118 950 9004

S

Grosvenor Casino
Queens Road
Sheffield
S2 4DF
Tel: 0114 275 7433
Fax: 0114 272 3667

Bonaparte's Casino Club
17 Livesey Street
Sheffield
S6 2BL
Tel: 0114 285 5566
Fax: 0114 285 2758

Ladbroke Casino
59 Wellington Street
Stockport
SK1 3AD
Tel: 0161 480 3037
Fax: 0161 480 7853

Ladbroke Casino
Aintree Oval Road
Teesside Leisure Park
Stockton-on-Tees
TS17 7BH
Tel: 01642 603030
Fax: 01642 606000

Stanley Churchill's Casino
14–16 Broad Street
Hanley
Stoke on Trent
ST1 4FU
Tel: 01782 213 499
Fax: 01782 283 611

Grosvenor Casino
11 Cranbury Terrace
Southampton
SO14 0LH
Tel: 023 80 636 955
Fax: 023 80 634 305

Grosvenor Sporting Club
1a North Bridge Street
Sunderland
SR5 1AD
Tel: 0191 514 5551

Grosvenor Casino
Northampton Lane
Swansea
SA1 4EH
Tel: 01792 651 799
Fax: 01792 652 889

T

Torquay Casino Club
Abbey Road
Torquay
TQ2 5NR
Tel: 01803 294 901
Fax: 01803 291 261

W

Stanley Walsall Casino
8-9 Stafford Street
Walsall
WS2 8DG
Tel: 01922 613 244
Fax: 01922 725 527

The Grosvenor Casino
Bentley Mill Way
Walsall
WS2 0LE
Tel: 01922 645222
Fax: 01922 645007

Europe

All European casinos are listed alphabetically in terms of the country.

Austria

Concord Card Casino, 1110
Vienna, Brehmstrasse 21,
Vienna,
Austria.
Tel: ++43 (1) 749-0136

This is one of the foremost venues in Europe and hosts European ranking tournaments.

Casino Austria,
Im Kurpack,
Kaiser Franz Ring 1,
A-2500 Baden bei Wein,
Baden,
Austria.
Tel: ++43 (0) 2252-444-96 119

Casino Austria,
Symphonikerplatz 3,
A- 6900, Bregenz, 6900,
Austria.
Tel: ++43 (0) 5574-45-127

Concord Card Casino,
Kärntnerstr.9,
A- 8020, Graz,
Austria.
Tel: ++43 (0) 316-707-770

Airport Poker Casino,
Kranebitter Allee 88,
Innsbruck,
6020, Austria.
Tel: ++43 (1) 512 28 1863

Casino Royal,
6020 Innsbruck,
Amraserstr.6,
Innsbruck, Austria.
Tel: ++43 (0) 512-584-747

Casinos Austria,
Hotel Goldener Greif,
Hinderstadt,
A-6370, Kitzbühel,
Austria.
Tel: ++43 (0) 5356-623-00

Casinos Austria,
Schloss Klessheim,
5071 Wals-Siezenheim,
Salzburg,
Austria.
Tel: ++43 (0) 662-8544-550

Casinos Austria,
A-6100 Seefeld/Tirol,
Bahnhofstraße 124,
Seefeld,
Austria.
Tel: ++43 (0) 5212-2340

Casinos Austria,
A-9220 Velden,
AM Corso 17,
Velden,
Austria.
Tel: ++43 (0) 4274-2064

Casinos Austria,
Palais Esterházy,
Kärntner Strasse 41,
A-1010, Vienna,
Austria.
Tel: ++43 (0) 1-512-48-36

Poker World,
Franzosengraben 3 – 5,
A-1030, Vienna,
Austria.
Tel: ++43 (0) 1 796-9933

Denmark

Casino Marienlyst,
Ndr. Strandvej 2, 3000 Helsingör,
Copenhagen,
Denmark.
Tel: ++45 49 28 01 57

Royal Scandinavian Casino,
Store Torv 4,
8000 Aarhus C,
Aarhus,
Denmark.
Tel: ++45 (0) 86192-122

Finland

Casino Ray,
Ramada Presidentti Hotel,
Etelaeinen Rautatiekatu 4, 00100,
Helsinki, Finland.
Tel: ++358 (0) 9-680-800

France

Aviation Club de France,
104 Champs Elysees,
Paris,
France.
Tel: ++33 (0) 1-4562-2688

Germany

Spiel Bad Aachen,
44 Monheimsallee,
Kurpack,
Bad Aachen,
D-52062,
Germany.
Tel: ++49 (0) 241 18080

Spiel Casino Niedersachen,
Ochtruper str.38,
PO Box 159,
D- 48455 Bad Bentheim,
Niedersachen,
Germany.
Tel: ++49 (0) 5922-98760

Spielbank Bad Kissingen,
Im Liutpold-Park,
PO Box 1164,
D-97688,
Bad Kissingen, Germany.
Tel: ++49 (0) 971 2031

Spiel Bad Oeynhausen,
Staatlichens Kurhaus im Kurpark,
D-32545,
Bad Oeynhausen,
Germany.
Tel: ++49 (0) 5731 18080

Spielbank Bad Zwischenahn,
Im Jagdhaus Eiden Hotel,
Lagdhaus Eiden am See,
D-2903,
Bad Zwischenahn,
Germany.
Tel: ++49 (0) 4403 9380-0

Spielbank Baden Baden,
Kaiseralle 1,
Baden-Baden,
Germany.
Tel: ++49 0 72-21 21060

Spielbank Berlin,
Budapester str,
Europa Center,
D-1000,
Berlin 30,
Germany.
Tel: ++49 (0) 30 261 1501

Spielbank Bremen,
Bottcherstraße 3-5,
D–28195,
Bremen,
Germany.
Tel: ++49 (0) 421 329000

Spielbank Hohensybyrg,
Hohensyburg str 200,
D–44265,
Dortmund,
Germany.
Tel: ++49 (0) 231 774 0107

Spielbank Bayerische,
Am Kurpark,
PO Box 1243,
D-82467,
Garmisch-Partenkirchen,
Germany.
Tel: ++49 (0) 8821- 53090

Spielbank Hamburg,
Im Kurpack,
PO Box 2307,
D-61348,
Hamburg,
Germany.
Tel: ++49 (0) 6172 17010

Spielbank Kassel,
Bottcherstasse,
D-34131,
Kassel,
Germany.
Tel: ++49 (0) 5619 30850

Spielbank Konstanz,
Seestrasse 21,
D-78464,
Konstanz,
Germany.
Tel: ++49 (0) 7531 81570

Spielbank Schenefeld,
Industriesstr.1,
D-22869,
Schenefeld,
Germany.
Tel: ++49 (0) 40 83 90020

Spielbank Wiesbaden,
Kurhausplatz 1,
D-65189,
Wiesbaden,
Germany.
Tel: ++49 (0) 611 536 179

Greece

Casino Magic,
PO Box 412,
Xanthi,
671000,
Greece.Tel: ++30 541 70 900

Holland

Holland Casino,
Lido,
Max Euweplein 62,
1017MB, Amsterdam,
1017MC,
Holland.
Tel: ++31 (0) 20-521-1111

Russia

Cosmos Casino Poker Club,
Prospect Mira 150,
Moscow,
Russia.
Tel: ++7 095 234 1155

Taleon Club,
59 Moika Emb.,
St Petersburg,
191–183,
Russia.

Slovenia

Hit Casino,
Delpinova 5,
Nova Gorica,
Slovenia.
Tel: ++386 65-126-2341

Sweden

Kortoxens,
St Eriksgatan 60,
Stockholm,
Sweden.
Tel: ++46 8 651 00 48

The USA

There are too many casinos and card rooms in the USA even to mention or list. However, I will give a selection of the most well known venues, trying to include those in major cities.

Las Vegas

Las Vegas (amusingly pronounced Loss Vegas by many locals) has for the last 50 years been an oasis for both the high life and high-stakes poker. It is often considered the adults' Disneyland, especially so in the last decade with the development of capital and building projects which are on a truly monumental scale. Surprisingly, Las Vegas (often shortened to Vegas) has become increasingly popular in spite of recent changes in US legislation which now allows gaming in many other states.

Notwithstanding the exploitation of gaming elsewhere in the USA, Las Vegas remains the Mecca for all poker players from across the world. Las Vegas is a strange and heady mix of the glitz and glamour juxtaposed with the downright seedy. Nevertheless, Las Vegas' citizens have perfected the skills of playing and dealing poker. They have made an art form of it, so my advice is to take trip to Vegas. Every poker player should go at least once in their life.

The Vegas Machine is fine-tuned. They have honed to perfection the art of separating punters from their money and, believe me, it is always service with a smile (well, nearly always).

Binion's Horseshoe Casino

Binion's Horseshoe Casino, situated in downtown Las Vegas, provides a setting for the highest-stake gambling games in the world. A famous policy at Binion's is that you can bet any amount provided it is not greater than your initial bet. In other words, your first bet sets your limit and the limit the casino will play to. As a result they have some very high limits. In addition, for one month of every year, Binion's plays host to the biggest festival of poker in the world, namely the World Series of Poker.

Everyone who is anyone in the world of poker eventually makes their way to Binion's Horseshoe. It is quite simply the players' choice.

Binion's Horseshoe Casino
128 East Fremont
Las Vegas, NV 89101
United States
Tel: LV 702-382-1600
Website: http://www.binions.com

Other US Card Rooms

Isleta Gaming Palace
11000 Broadway SE,
Albuquerque,
NM 87105,
United States.
Tel: [1] 505-869-2614

Bally's Park Place
Park Place & Boardwalk,
Atlantic City,
NJ 08401,
United States.
Tel: [1] 609-340-2000
Toll-Free: 1-800-772-7777

Caesar's Atlantic City
2100 Pacific Avenue,
Atlantic City,
NJ 08401,
United States.
Tel: [1] 609-348-4411
Toll-Free: 1-800-223-7277

Harrah's Casino New Jersey
777 Harrah's Blvd,
Atlantic City,
NJ 08401,
United States.
Tel: [1] 609-441-5000
Toll-Free: 1-800-242-7724

Casino Rouge
1717 River Road North,
Baton Rouge,
LA 70802,
United States.
Tel:[1] 504-381-7777
Toll-Free: 1-800-447-6843

Christo's Card Room
110 S Samish,
Bellingham,
WA 98226,
United States.
Tel: [1] 360 738 1888

Lady Luck Casino Bettendorf
1821 State Street,
Bettendorf,
IA 52722,
United States.
Tel: [1] 319-359-7280
Toll-Free: 1-800-724-5825

Grand Casino Biloxi
265 Beach Blvd,
Biloxi,
MS 39530,
United States.
Tel: [1] 228-436-2946
Toll-Free: 1-800-946-2946

Harrah's East Chicago Casino
777 Harrah's Blvd,
East Chicago,
IN 46312,
United States
Tel: [1] 219-378-3000
Toll-Free: 1-800-HARRAHS

Crystal Park Casino Hotel
123 E.Artesia Blvd,
Compton (Los Angeles),
CA 90220,
United States.
Tel: [1] 310-631-3838
Toll-Free: 1-800-717-1000

Historic Franklin Hotel
700 Main Street,
Deadwood,
SD 57732,
United States.
Tel: [1] 605-578-2241
Toll-Free: 1-800-688-1876

Kickapoo Lucky Eagle Casino
Rt 1 Lucky Eagle Road,
Eagle Pass,
TX 78852,
United States.
Tel: [1] 830-758-1936
Toll-Free: 1-888-255-8259

Ceasar's Indiana
11999 Avenue of the Emperors,
Elizabeth,
IN 47117,
United States.
Tel: [1] 812-738-3848
Toll-Free: 1-888-ROMAN4U

Klondike Casino
309 4th Street,
Eureka,
CA 95501,
United States.
Tel: [1] 707-444-4633

Lake Bowl Card Room
511 East Bidwell Street,
Folsom,
CA 95630,
United States.
Tel: [1] 916-983-6000

Catfish Bend Riverboat Casino
902 Riverview Drive,
Fort Madison,
IA 52627,
United States.
Tel: [1] 319-753-2946

Lone Star Casino
Casino Avenue,
Fort Thompson,
SD 57339,
United States.
Tel: [1] 605-245-6000

Flamingo Casino-Kansas City
1800 East Front Street,
Kansas City,
MO 64120,
United States.
Tel: [1] 816-855-7777
Toll-Free: 1-800-946-8711

Grand Casino Coushatta
77 Coushatta Dr,
Kinder,
LA 70648,
United States.
Tel: [1] 337-378-1370
Toll-Free: 1-800-584-7263

Circus Circus
2880 Las Vegas Blvd South,
Las Vegas,
NV 89109,
United States.
Tel: [1] 702-734-0410
Toll-Free: 1-800-634-3450

Excalibur Hotel & Casino
3850 Las Vegas Blvd South,
Las Vegas,
NV 89119,
United States.
Tel: [1] 702-597-7777
Toll-Free: 1-800-937-7777

Frontier Poker Room
3120 Las Vegas Blvd South,
Las Vegas,
NV,
United States.
Tel: [1] 702-794-8200

Harrah's Las Vegas
3475 Las Vegas Blvd South,
Las Vegas,
NV 89109,
United States.
Tel: [1] 702-369-5000
Toll-Free: 1-800-HARRAHS

Edgewater Hotel & Casino
2020 South Casino Drive,
Laughlin,
NV 89028,
United States.
Tel: [1] 702-298-2453
Toll-Free: 1-800-677-4837

Bicycle Casino
7301 Eastern Avenue,
Bell Gardens,
South of Downtown,
710/ Florence,
Los Angeles,
CA 90201,
United States.
Tel: [1] 562-806-4646

Commerce Casino
6131 East Telegraph Road,
Commerce,
Los Angeles,
CA 90040,
United States.
Tel: [1] 323-721-2100

Hawaiian Gardens Casino
11871 Carson Street,
Hawaiian Gardens,
Los Angeles,
CA,
United States.
Tel: [1] 562-860-5887

Foxwood's Resort Casino
Route 2,
Mashantucket,
CT 06106,
United States.
Tel: [1] 860-312-3000
Toll-Free: (1) 800-48-POKER

Grand River Casino
Highway 20,
Mobridge,
SD 57601,
United States.
Tel: [1] 605-845-7104
Toll-Free: 1-800-475-3321

Harrah's Phoenix AK-Chin Casino
15406 Maricopa Road,
Maricopa,
AZ 85239,
United States.
Tel: [1] 480-802-5000
Toll-Free: (1) 800-427-7247

Harrah's Prairie Band Casino
12305 150th Road,
Mayetta,
KS 66509,
United States.
Tel: [1] 785-966-7777
Toll-Free: 1-800-HARRAHS

Harrah's Casino New Orleans
512 South Peters Rd,
New Orleans,
LA 70130,
United States.
Tel: [1] 504-533-6000

Harvey's Resort Hotel & Casino
Highway 50,
Lake Tahoe,
NV 89449,
United States.
Tel: [1] 775-588-2411
Toll-Free: 1-800-427-8397

Harvey's Wagon Wheel Hotel &
Casino
321 Gregory Street,
Central City,
CO 80427,
United States.
Tel: [1] 303-582-0800
Toll-Free: 1-800-924-6646

Bally's Casino Lakeshore Resort
1 Stars & Stripes Blvd,
New Orleans,
LA,
United States.
Tel: [1] 504-248-3200
Toll-Free: 1-800-57-BALLY

Casino Omaha
1 Blackbird Bend,
Onawa,
IA 51040,
United States.
Tel: [1] 712-423-3700
Toll-Free: 1-800-858-8238

Atlantis Casino
3800 South Virginia Street,
Reno,
NV 89502,
United States.
Tel: [1] 775-825-4700
Toll-Free: 1-800-723-6500

Circus Circus Hotel and Casino
500 North Sierra Street,
Reno,
NV 89503,
United States.
Tel: [1] 775-329-0711
Toll-Free: 1-800-648-5010

Gold Strike Casino Resort
1010 Casino Center Drive,
Robinsonville,
MS 38664,
United States.
Tel: [1] 662-357-1111
Toll-Free: 1-888-24K-STAY

Duffy's Card Room & Casino
1944 El Camino Avenue,
Sacramento,
CA 95815,
United States.
Tel: [1] 916-920-5809

Ladbroke's Casino San Pablo
13255 San Pablo Ave,
San Pablo (San Francisco),
CA 94806,
United States.
Tel: [1] 510-215-7888

City of Gold Casino
10-B City of Gold Road,
Santa Fe,
NM 87501,
United States.
Tel: [1] 505-455-3313
Toll-Free: 1-800-455-3313

Hideaway Card Room
14502 Aurora North,
Seattle,
WA 98133,
United States.
Tel: [1] 206-362-9494

Comstock Card Room
125 West 11th Street,
Tracey,
CA 95376,
United States.
Tel: [1] 209-832-1111

Ameristar Casino
4146 Washington Street,
Vicksburg,
MS,
United States.
Tel: [1] 662-638-1000
Toll-Free: 1-800-700-7456

Quiz

**Gambling is the surest way of getting
nothing for something.**
Wilson Mizner

This brief chapter is an attempt to allow you to test your newly acquired knowledge of poker. Remember there are seldom any absolutely right answers and often a range of different options will all work just as well as each other. For this reason, there will often be more than one answer to each question. Here, Brian has set the questions and John and Barry have each indicated what they would do in each scenario.

Question 1

The scenario is the final table of a pot-limit Hold 'Em tournament, you are in mid-position and play is about to come to you. You hold A-A and are wondering about a raise. You are attentive to all that is happening at the table and notice that a player to act behind you is looking alert suddenly and has lifted a pile of chips. What do you do?

John:

You do not raise with your two aces as it is fairly obvious that the player behind you is about to raise. The correct play is to just call, let the other player raise and then re-raise or just flat call when the action gets back to you. You could make your choice on the re-raise or flat call depending on whether other players call, what your chip position is, what the chip position of the other callers is etc. If there is one or more other callers, you should probably re-raise but if there is only the original raiser you might want to just call hoping to trap the player into betting again. I would probably re-raise again anyway; it is the safer option.

Barry:

I agree with John's answer. However, note that some players, if they have a medium-strength hand, will grab their chips as a defence mechanism to try to stop opponents betting. You just have to judge your player.

Question 2

The scenario is again the final table of a pot-limit Hold 'Em tournament, you are in mid-position and the action is just about to come to you. This time, however, you hold 10-10 and are wondering about a raise. You notice that a player to act behind you is suddenly alert and has lifted a pile of chips. What do you do this time?

John:

Here you have an entirely different proposition. It is obvious that your opponent has a good hand. The following hands are likely to be what your opponent is holding, as very few others will make a player sit up and take notice:

i)   A high pair such as A-A, K-K or Q-Q (J-J is also possible but much less likely).

ii) Two high cards such as A-K or A-Q.

What I like to do in these situations is think in terms of the percentage chance of a holding. The percentage chance of holding either the high pair or the two high cards is worked out as follows. There are 6 two-card combinations possible for each high pair (e.g. A♠A♥, A♠A♦, A♠A♣, A♥A♦, A♥A♣, A♦A♣) making 18 possibilities in all for the three high pairs. There are 16 two-card combinations which make A-K (e.g. A♠K♠, A♠K♥, A♠K♦, A♠K♣ etc.) and 16 for A-Q, making 32 in all. If you were sure that these are the only combinations then it is 18 chances in 50 (or 36 per cent) that your opponent holds a high pair and 32 chances in 50 (64 per cent) that it is two high cards.

When your opponent has a high pair, you are definitely the underdog (you only have an approximate 17 per cent chance of winning). When your opponent has two high cards, your chance of winning is some 52 per cent. Thus, for every 100 times you play your 10-10 win against these holdings about 40 times (36 x 17 per cent plus 64 x 52 per cent). The odds are 6/4 against you winning.

So what should you do? I would pass the hand, unless my opponent has very few chips left and/or I have a big stack, then I might, just might, play the hand against him.

Incidentally, you cannot hope to undertake this type of analysis at the table. It has to be done as part of your preparation work. Once you understand the principle it is easy enough to analyse similar situations.

Barry:

I agree again, but if the blinds were high enough and I was on a short stack (or he was) I would raise anyway to shut out the rest of the field.

Question 3

The scenario is the same as the previous two questions. This time, however, you hold Q-Q and are wondering about a raise. The player to act behind you is suddenly alert and has lifted a pile of chips. What do you do this time?

John:

The analysis is similar to the previous question. You take it as certain (or nearly certain) that your opponent has a very good hand. The following hands are likely to be what your opponent is holding:

i)   A high pair, A-A or K-K.
ii) Two high cards, A-K or A-Q.
iii) A small pair – perhaps J-J? Well, maybe if it's a poor player, but I doubt it.

You can exercise your brain by working out the chance of holding each and hence the overall chance of your opponent winning by following the procedure in the last example. So what should you do? Here again, I would *perhaps* pass the hand but I would have to be very sure of my read on the opponent and once again it would depend on our relative chip positions. Maybe, however, it would better to call and see if the opponent does in fact raise, then you could make your decision.

Barry:

Here I differ from John. I would definitely raise with two queens in this situation. It is by no means certain that the other player has one of the hands noted above. Other possibilities could be A-J, A-10, K-Q suited or small pairs like 10-10 or 9-9. If you raise, the opponent will perhaps pass these hands. It is often the case that the player who gets the chips into the pot first wins, so you can sometimes become favourite simply by betting out first. (Incidentally this is an example of position working in reverse.)

Question 4

You are at the final table of a pot-limit Hold 'Em tournament and are last to act. There is one other player with about the same number of chips as you. Your opponent has called your speculative raise before the flop and has now checked to you. You hold [A♣] [9♣] and the flop is [J♣] [10♣] [9♦]. What do you do this time?

John:

This one is not clear-cut and depends on a number of factors. You have a reasonable drawing hand, which could improve to a flush, two pair or trips. However, the flop looks dangerous. Your opponent could conceivably be slow playing K-Q or he may have [J♠] [10♠] and I would not rule out K-J or even Q-Q. Against all of these possible holdings, you are the underdog, so I would advise cautious play and just check along. Of course, if the flop had been [J♣] [9♦] [3♣] this would be an entirely different proposition as I would have second top pair and flush draw against one opponent. Here, I may well bet hoping to get the pot there and then. Notice that the range of danger hands your opponent is likely to hold has decreased markedly. Two pair is very unlikely so the only real danger is if your opponent holds something like K-J or Q-Q. However, the check in this case indicates weakness. If your opponent held one of these two cards he would surely bet to stop you getting a free draw at a possible flush. So I would probably bet.

Barry:

I disagree with John. I would get my chips all-in without hesitation. Against J-10 you are about evens (you can win with a club, ace or 9). You have the best draw so even against K-Q you've still got a 1 in 3 chance of winning (odds of 2/1 against).

Question 5

The scenario is the same as in question 4 except it is at an early stage of a re-buy tournament and you can afford to re-buy. You are holding A♠ 9♣ to a J♣ 10♠ 9♦ flop. What do you do?

John:

I would bet my drawing hand (this is a semi-bluff) hoping to win the pot outright but knowing that if I am called or raised I still have a chance of winning and all that the play will cost me is a re-buy. I will not be out of the tournament as in the previous example. If I win the pot here it will help to build my stack of chips which is arguably a more important strategy than trying to limit the number of buy-ins you have.

Barry:

Barry's answer is the same as in Question 4.

Question 6

At an early stage of a re-buy tournament you are holding [A♣] [9♣] to a [J♣] [10♣] [8♦] flop. What do you do?

John:

You have a strong drawing hand with any club, Q or 7 helping your hand. I would bet hoping to win the pot outright but knowing if I am called I still have plenty of outs. Again, I would be more cautious in the latter stages of a tournament where I may just check and see what develops.

Barry:

Get all-in as quickly as possible. Then shout for a buy-in when you miss all your draws and your opponent's K-J holds up.

Question 7

You hold [9♦] [8♦] early in a tournament and there has been a raise with three callers, you are last to act. What do you do?

John:

The [9♦] [8♦] is not a great hand, despite what other commentators may say, but in this situation it is worth playing. You are hoping to get any of the following flops: A-9-8, where an opponent with an ace and a high card can be trapped; 8-7-6, a reasonable draw if you can re-buy; or even 8-3-2 may be good. However, I would be reluctant to call with a hand like [9♦] [8♦] late in a tournament no matter how many other callers there are. It's too risky. In good position I might make a small raise, hoping that everyone will pass but realising that if I am called I could still be OK in the pot.

Barry:

I would call as long as it was for a small percentage of my stack. I agree that the main danger is catching a small piece of the flop (i.e. getting top pair with bad kicker) and becoming committed to it.

Question 8

You hold [4♣] [4♠] and the flop comes [7♦] [4♦] [4♥]. What do you do?

John and Barry agree:

You have the deck 'crippled' unless someone holds 7-7 in hand. Therefore, you check to let your opponents catch up and maybe get a flush or straight. That way you may get a call eventually.

Question 9

You hold [4♣] [4♠] and the flop comes [7♦] [7♠] [4♥]. What do you do?

John:

You bet like fury in the hope that someone has a 7. You might even be extremely lucky and two other players could each hold a 7. Against two players, holding A-7 and 8-7 respectively, your hand has about a 70 per cent chance of winning. An ace or an eight or a running pair needs to come in the last two cards for you to lose. Incidentally, if you had 7-7 and the flop was 7-4-4 you would not bet as you have an extremely strong hand and wouldn't care if the other players improve their hands, indeed you would want them to improve.

Barry:

I more or less agree with John, but I would be tempted to check against only one other player. Also, note that an A-A-4 is a much better flop for you in this position, as people tend to play aces more often than 7s.

Question 10

It is down to the last two in a pot-limit tournament; you have chips to the value of 5000 points and your opponent has chips of 85,000 value. The blinds are now 1000 for each player, so there are 2000 chips in the pot and you are facing a raise of 2000. You hold 10♠ 7♠. What do you do?

John and Barry agree:

This is a dire situation for you. Your opponent is likely to be raising with almost any holding, hoping to drive you off, but you cannot keep passing even bad hands or you will be anted away (i.e. the cost of the blinds will eat away your chips). You might be able to pass just one or two more times in the hope of getting, say, an A-x so that you can make a stand. On the other hand, it is probably best to take a chance and call with the 10♠ 7♠. If you held J-10 or better instead then the best course would probably be to raise all-in. Incidentally, in the second series of *Late Night Poker*, Debbie Berlin had a similarly abysmal chip position against Ross Boatman but turned it around and went on to win her heat. So don't give up hope, even if your opponent is a huge chip leader, because things can change very fast.

Question 11

You are one of two players remaining in a pot-limit tournament. You have 25,000 in chips and your opponent has chips of 75,000 value. The blinds are now 4000 for each player so there are 8000 chips in the pot and you are facing a raise of 8000. You hold 2-2 (a pair of ducks). What do you do?

John:

You have 21,000 left after your blind so you call the 8000 bet and raise the other 13,000 all-in. Your opponent's most likely holding is two higher cards such as K-Q or even K-9 if he is an aggressive player. The raise may win you the pot immediately, but if not you are a better than even money chance against two high cards (it's about 10/11 on the 2-2 hand). If you are unlucky enough to run into a higher pair, well, you are dead in the water, but these are the risks you must take in tournament poker.

Barry:

It's a close decision but I would pass. You do not have enough chips to get your opponent to fold. Your options are to sit on the 21,000 that you have or play out a 50,000 pot. It is not unreasonable to credit your opponent with a pair 20 per cent of the time he raises, in which case you are a big underdog. The rest of the time you are just slightly better than even money. However, if my pair was higher, even say 5-5, I would go all-in because there is now a chance that my opponent could be playing something like A-4 or A-3, which is only one overcard.

Question 12

The scenario is the same as before: it is down to the last two in a pot-limit tournament; you have 25,000 in chips while your opponent has chips of 75,000; the blinds are now 4000 for each player making a pot of 8000 chips; and you are facing a raise of 8000. This time, however, you hold K-K (a pair of kings). What do you do?

John:

You could raise all-in to try to win the pot immediately. However, you might take a risk and just call hoping that after the flop your opponent will bet, or call your bet, and you will double through your chips. If you win this pot, the total chips would be split 50:50 and you would be back in contention for the tournament. The risk you are taking is that your opponent has something like an A-x and that an ace comes on the flop, but you sometimes just have to take the risk. Incidentally, say you do just flat call the 8000 raise and an ace does come on the flop, you are forced to bet or call because your opponent may not have an ace and there is too much in the pot for you to pass with a holding of K-K.

Barry:

Since your opponent is very unlikely to fold, you might as well get all of your chips in the pot while you are a big favourite and avoid the danger of being bluffed out on the flop should an ace fall. If both players had an extra 50,000 each, however, making the relative chip positions more even, I would be tempted to just call and try to get my opponent to make a big move on the flop (i.e.

bluff or semi-bluff). If you do just call, keep your fingers crossed that an ace does not show up.

Having thought about these questions and perhaps come up with your own answers before examining ours, I hope you will agree that even the simplest situation can be approached in more than one way and that there is seldom only one solution to a particular situation. But that's the nature of poker and it is what makes the game so interesting.

Glossary

He would cut the cards even if he was playing poker with his mother.
Jimmy Carter

A

Ace-High:	A hand having an ace but no pair.
Aces Up:	Two pair, the highest pair being aces.
Action:	The act of putting chips in the pot, gambling of any sort.
Action Player:	A player who gives a lot of action, also called a 'loose' player.
Active Player:	Any player still in the hand, competing for the pot.
Act out of Turn:	A player attempting to bet or raise prior to his turn to act.
Advertise:	To bluff and then show the hand to other players in the hope that they will call sometime later when you have a legitimate hand.
All-in:	All your money or chips in the pot.
Ante:	An agreed nominal bet required from each player before the start of a hand.

B

Babies:	Small cards – a 2, 3, 4 or 5.
Back Door:	To back door a flush or straight is when the last two cards make a player's hand, even though this was not the original hand the player was drawing to.
Bad Beat:	When a strong hand is outdrawn by a weaker hand, considered to be held by a player who got lucky.
Bankroll:	A player's total stake money.
Best Hand:	The one that takes the pot.
Bet:	To intentionally put chips into the pot.
Bet Blind:	To wager without looking at one's hole cards.
Bet Half the Pot:	To bet half the amount of the pot. Half the pot is the maximum allowable bet in some UK home games.
Bet in the Dark:	To bet before seeing the next or any cards.
Bet Into:	To make a bet looking at what seems to be a superior hand.
Bet the Pot:	To bet the amount of the pot. Pot limit is the usual maximum allowable bet in UK casino games.
Big Blind:	The small forced bet made by the player in second left position to the dealer button. It is made before any cards are dealt and is a live bet. Thus the player on the big blind can raise when the action gets back to him.
Big Slick:	Ace-king as the first two cards.
Blank:	A card that does not look like it has improved anyone's hand.
Blind:	A forced bet made by the two players to the dealer's left (or to the left of the dealer button). It is made before any cards are dealt and is a live bet.

Bluff:	To bet or raise with a poor hand in the hope that other players will pass and you will win the pot.
Board:	All five cards, in community card games, turned face up in the centre of the table.
Boxed Card:	A card facing the other way to the remaining cards in the deck.
Bullet:	Another name for an ace.
Burn:	To take a card from the top of the deck before dealing out the cards (it is an attempt to prevent cheating). This card is removed from play.
Button:	A disk used to indicate the player who would nominally be dealing if there were no house dealer.
Buy the Button:	A bet or raise which makes players behind you fold, making you the last to act in succeeding betting rounds.
Buy the Pot:	To bluff. (Usually a big bet at a small pot.)

C

Call:	To match the previous bet.
Calling Station:	A pejorative term for a player who perpetually calls and cannot be bluffed.
Cards Speak:	When the cards are laid face up on the table the correct reading of the hand will win the pot. That is, the highest hand will win the pot irrespective of what the player declares the hand to be. For instance, a player may not see that he has hit a flush and may declare something else, but it is the flush which will count.
Case Card:	The last card of a particular rank when the other three are already out.

Cash In: Take your chips and leave the game.

Check: To refrain from betting. This is often indicated by a player tapping the table. The player may still call or raise if another player bets.

Check Raise: To check and, if another player bets, to raise when the action gets back to you.

Chemmy Shuffle: Scrambling the cards face down on the table.

Cinch Hand: A hand that will win easily.

Clinic: A poker game where there are a lot of post-mortems about the hands that are played.

Closed Poker: Games such as draw poker where there are no community cards and all of the cards are dealt face down.

Coffee Housing: Talking in an attempt to mislead another player about the strength of a hand. For instance, a player holding A-A as their first two cards might say 'Let's gamble here,' implying a much weaker holding. Coffee housing is considered bad etiquette in the UK but not in the USA. This is also called 'speech play'.

Cold Call: To call a raised pot without having any prior investment in the pot.

Cold Deck: A deck that has been rigged by cheats. It will be cooler in temperature than the deck used in previous hands, as it has been concealed in the cheat's pocket and brought out when the 'mark' is to be cheated. The deck will be fixed to give the mark a good hand but the cheat will get a slightly better winning hand.

Collusion: Any act, including betting or raising, by two or more players in partnership in an attempt to cheat other players.

Colt 45: Reputedly the only thing that beats a royal flush.

Community Cards: The cards dealt face up in the centre of the table that are shared by all active players.

Connectors: Consecutive cards which could help make a straight, e.g. 6-7 or 10-J.

Counterfeit: When a card on the board duplicates one in your hand. For instance, you hold 10-J and the board is K-Q-3, but if a J comes on fourth street it counterfeits the one in your hand, making your hand worse as a result. Counterfeiting is common in high-low games.

Cripple the Deck: To have all of the cards that make up a good hand with a particular board. If you hold A-K, and the flop is A-A-K, you will have the deck crippled in that no one else can have a playable hand. If you bet you will not be called.

D

Dead Card: A card no longer in play.

Dead Hand: A hand no longer in play, perhaps due to some deviation from the rules.

Dead Man's Hand: Two black aces and two black 8s have become known as the dead man's hand because Wild Bill Hickock is reputed to have held the hand when he was shot in the back during a saloon poker hand in Deadwood, South Dakota.

Deal: To distribute the cards to each player.

Dealer: The player who is distributing the cards.

Dealer's Advantage: The dealer is last to act which is a big advantage.

Dealer's Choice: A game in which each dealer, in turn, chooses the type of poker to be played.

Deck: The standard pack of 52 playing cards.

Deuce: The 2 of any suit (also called a 'duck').

Dog: Americanism for the worst or underdog hand. Big dog is used for a big disadvantage and little dog for a small disadvantage.

Dog It: To play a hand which is good, slowly, in order not to chase the other players away. Similar to 'slow play'.

Door Card: The first card dealt face up in five- or seven-card stud.

Double Belly Buster: A hand with two inside straight draws. An example might be a flop containing 10-8-6, when you have 7-4 – a 9 or a 5 will make the hand into a straight. The odds of getting the straight from a double belly buster are the same as for an open-ended straight draw.

Down and Dirty: This expression is sometimes used while the final card at seven-card stud poker is being dealt. Its meaning is obscure.

Down Cards: The concealed cards. In Hold 'Em, the first two cards that are dealt to each player face down. Also called the 'hole cards'.

Down the River: All the way to the last card at seven stud, another name for seven-card stud.

Drawing Dead: Drawing to a hand that cannot possibly win. An example is drawing to a 4-flush when a full house is already out.

Drawing Hand: A potentially strong hand requiring a particular card/s from the draw to make it.

Draw Poker: A form of poker in which each player receives five cards and after the first round of betting has the option of discarding one or more of them and receiving new cards in their place.

Driving Seat: A player holding the best hand and making the betting.

Drowning: Losing heavily.

Duck: The two of any suit (also called a 'deuce').

E

Expectation: The average amount you make in a specific event or period. Thus, if you have won £7500 in the last 34 tournaments, your expectation per tournament is £7500 ÷ 34 which is £220. Conversely, if you have lost £1500 in the last 34 tournaments, your expectation per tournament is £1500 ÷ 34 or – £44.

F

False Cut: A cut which is not properly done.

Family Pot: A pot in which all or most of the players at the table are still involved at a particular point in the progress of a hand.

Fast Game: A game with a good pace of action and frequent heavy raises.

Fast Player: A heavy bettor; a frequent raiser.

Feeler Bet: A minimum bet made to test the strength of the other players' hands.

Fifth Street: The fifth and final community card on the board. In stud poker, it is the fifth card dealt to each player.

Fill Up: To draw cards and make your hand.

First Position: The player on the immediate left of the dealer. In Hold 'Em this player is first to act throughout the game.

Fish: This is a derogatory term used (mainly in the US) to describe a weak or losing player.

Flop: The first three community cards, which are turned face up together before the start of the second round of betting.

Flush: Five cards of the same suit.

Flush Draw: Having four cards of the same suit and hoping to draw a fifth to make a flush.

Fold: To lay down one's hand.

Fold Out of Turn: To fold prematurely.

Fourth Street: The fourth and final community card on the board. In stud poker, it is the fourth card dealt to each player.

Free Card: When all players check, the next card is seen without any money entering the pot. This card is a free card.

Free Roll: In Hold 'Em or other flop games where two players have the same hand, but one also has the chance of improving to a better hand. For instance, both may have A-K-Q-J-10 except one player has a flush draw and the other does not.

Freeze Out: A game or tournament in which all players start with the same amount and play until one player has won all the chips.

Friend: A card that assists or improves the hand.

Friendly Game: No such game.

Full House: Any three cards of the same rank, plus any pair of a different rank.

Full Table: At Hold 'Em, a table of 11 or 12 players.

G

Gambler: A player that bucks the odds.

Gap: The missing inside card that would make a straight.

Gut Shot: A card that will make a straight. An inside straight draw.

H

Hand:	A player's best five cards.
Head to Head:	Two players heads-up in a game of poker.
Heads-Up:	A game between just two players, often the remaining two players of a tournament.
High Roller:	A heavy bettor. One who plays for high stakes.
Hold 'Em:	A form of poker in which players use five community cards in combination with their two hole cards to form the best five-card hand. Also called Texas Hold 'Em.
Hole Cards:	The concealed cards. In Hold 'Em, the first two cards that are dealt to each player face down. Also called the 'down cards'.
Hot Seat:	The seat that has or had a run of winning hands.

I

Ignorant End:	The low end of a straight. For instance, if the flop in Hold 'Em is 9-8-7 the ignorant end straight would be the 6-5.
Inside Straight:	Four cards requiring one in the middle to fill a straight.
Insurance:	A side bet (usually when a large pot is involved) made between two players, but can also involve others.

K

Kibitzer:	A spectator, usually unappreciated by the players.
Kicker:	The second highest card in a hand. If the holding is A-9, the 9 is the kicker.

Kicker Trouble: When the second card is low, say a 7 or below, the player will have difficulty winning the pot if another player also holds the highest card because his kicker is liable to be bigger.

L

Lay Down: To fold one's hand. Often refers to folding a reasonably good hand.

Live Blind: When the player is allowed to raise even if no one else raises first.

Live Card: A card which has not yet been exposed.

Live One: Refers to a player who plays more hands than the game structure justifies.

Lock: The winning hand; a hand that is unbeatable.

Locked up: To hold a winning or unbeatable hand and have the pot as good as won. This phrase is also used to describe a player who has won a lot of chips and is very unlikely to lose them again. The player is said to have the chips locked up.

M

Main Pot: When a player puts all of his chips in the pot (goes all-in), that player is only eligible to win the pot consisting of the bets he was able to match. This is called the main pot. Additional bets are placed in a 'side pot' and are contested among the remaining players. The names main and side pots remain irrespective of which contains the most chips.

Maniac: An American expression meaning a very aggressive player who plays lots of hands and raises often. This type of player seems to bet and raise with very weak hands.

Mechanic: A card cheat.

Miscall: An error made when announcing one's hand. (See also Cards Speak).

Monkey: £500.

Move-In: To move all your chips into the pot in a no-limit game.

Muck: To discard or throw away a hand. Also refers to all dead cards in the discard heap.

N

No-Limit Poker: A game in which players can bet up to the amount they have in front of them on any given betting round, irrespective of the amount of chips in the pot. Also called 'table stakes'.

Nut Flush: The best available flush.

Nuts: The best possible hand at any point in the game; a cinch hand.

O

Offsuit: Term used to describe the first two cards if they are of different suits.

Omaha: A flop game similar to Hold 'Em, but where each player is dealt four cards instead of two. In Omaha, a hand must be made using exactly two pocket cards, plus three from the table.

One Way Action: When only one player is in against you.

On Tilt: Becoming emotionally upset and hence playing poorly.

Open-ended Straight Draw: Four consecutive cards requiring one at either end to make a straight.

Open Poker: Games where some of the cards are dealt face up.

Out: A card remaining in the deck that improves your hand.

Outdraw: To beat an opponent by drawing a card or cards to improve a lesser hand into a winner.

Out of Turn: Not in proper sequence.

Overpair: A pair higher than any card on the board. If a player holds K-K and the flop comes Q-10-3, that player has an overpair.

P

Pair: Two cards of the same rank.

Pass: Fold.

Pat Hand: A hand which is complete, usually refers to games such as draw poker.

Play Over: An American term and concept meaning to temporarily play in the seat of an absent player. A transparent box is placed over the chips of the absent player.

Pony: £25.

Position: Your seat in relation to the dealer, and thus your place in the betting order.

Pot: The money or chips in the centre of the table.

Pot Limit: A game in which the maximum bet is the total in the pot at the time of betting. The limit used in most UK casino games.

Pot Odds: The amount of money in the pot divided by the amount of money it will cost you to continue in the hand. If there is £300 in the pot and it costs you £120 to call the bet you are getting pot odds of 300/120 or 5/2.

Protect Your Hand (1):   To place a chip or chips on your cards to prevent them from being accidentally discarded by the dealer.

Protect Your Hand (2):   A bet to protect the money you have already put in a pot. Also called 'defending your hand' e.g. protecting/defending the Big Blind means to put an extra small bet into the pot no matter how bad your hand is.

Put a Player On: To guess or otherwise determine an opponent's hand and play accordingly.

Q

Quads: Four of a kind.

R

Rag: A card which is small and appears to help no one.

Rag Off: To get a final card that doesn't help you.

Ragged Flop: Flop cards that are seemingly of no use to any player's hand.

Rags: Worthless cards. Blanks.

Rail: The sideline around a poker table or playing area.

Railbird: A non-playing spectator or kibitzer. The term is often used pejoratively to describe an ex-player who has lost and is now out of the game.

Rainbow Flop: A flop with three different suits.

Raise: To call and increase the previous bet.

Rake: In the USA and in some European countries, the casino/house makes a charge by taking a fixed percentage from each pot. In the UK, charges are made by the hour for the seat.

Random Card: A card selected from a group of unknown cards not yet in play which have an equal chance of being chosen.

Random Card Concept: The substitution of a random card for a player's proper card which he may be unable to receive for any reason, leaves the player with the same mathematical chances of winning the pot before the irregularity occurred. It is therefore assumed that the player has not been materially injured.

Rank: The value of a card. Each card has a suit and a rank. The [10♠] and [10♦] are two cards of the same rank.

Rat Hole: To pocket part of one's table stakes secretly. It is considered unethical to take money off the playing surface.

Read: To try and determine, using logical deduction, your opponent's cards or betting strategy.

Re-buy: An additional entry fee in tournament play. When a player loses all his chips, a re-buy is allowed in some types of competitions for a fixed period of time, usually about 1½ – 2 hours.

Represent: To bet in a way that suggests you are holding a strong hand. For example, if the flop comes A-J-3 and you hold 9-9 and have bet before the flop, you might also bet on the flop hoping that the other players will think you have an ace (you are representing an ace).

Re-raise: To raise a raise.

Ring Game: A game with nine to eleven players, the optimum size at Hold 'Em poker.

River: The last community card on the board, also called fifth street.

Rock: A very conservative and tight player.

Rock Garden: A table populated with rocks.

Roll: A winning streak.

Rolled Up: A term indicating the first three cards at seven stud all of the same rank.

Rounder: A poker player, usually professional, who does the rounds of poker games in the area or country. Playing in Glasgow on Monday, Newcastle on Tuesday, back to Glasgow on Wednesday and then on to Dundee on Thursday is an example of a rounder's schedule.

Round of Betting: The period during which each active player has the right to check, bet or raise. It ends when the last bet or raise has been called by all players still in the hand.

Royal Flush: The best possible poker hand, consisting of 10-J-Q-K-A, all of the same suit.

Run: A straight; sometimes also refers to a series of hands.

Running Pair: Two cards of the same rank that fall consecutively, usually on fourth and fifth street in Hold 'Em or Omaha.

Rush: A winning streak.

S

Satellite: A small-stakes tournament where the winner(s) gains entry into a bigger tournament. (A super satellite is where there is a very small entry and the winner(s) gains entry into a very big tournament.)

Scare Card: A card which could make your hand a loser. For example, if you held Q-Q and the flop is A-6-3, then the ace is a scare card for you.

See: To call.

Sell Your Hand: Make a small bet with a strong hand, hoping to get a call. Usually made when you think a bigger bet would make your opponents pass.

Semi-Bluff: To bet with a hand which isn't the best hand, but which has a reasonable chance of improving. This term was first coined by David Sklansky.

Set: Usually refers to three of a kind or trips where the pair in a player's hand matches a card on the board. Can also be used in the context of four of a kind, i.e. a set of quads.

Shill: An American term and concept where a casino employee sits in on a game to keep it going. This is not allowed in the UK and is not known in Europe.

Shiner: A mirror or other reflective object used by cheats in an attempt to see hidden cards as they are dealt. In home or self-dealt games, the player may wear a ring with a reflective surface.

Showdown: The process of determining who has the best hand after all cards are dealt and all bets are completed.

Shuffle: Mixing of the cards before and between deals.

Side Pot: A separate pot contested by other players when one player is all-in.

Slow Play: To bet less than the strength of the hand would normally deserve in order to get more players into the pot and to deceive other players about the strength of your hand.

Snake Eyes: A pair of aces.

Soft Play Agreement: This is where a player bets less than they normally would or checks good hands when against friends, husbands or wives. It is not prohibited, but is unethical.

Speech Play: See Coffee Housing.

Speeding Around: Playing loose for one period and then tight for another with no definable pattern.

Splash the Pot: To throw your chips into the pot instead of placing them in front of you. This makes it difficult for the dealer to determine the amount of the bet.

Split: A tie.

Split Pot: A pot in which two or more hands are equal, and the pot is shared.

Stack: The pile of chips in front of a player.

Standard Deck: A deck of cards having four suits with thirteen cards to each suit.

Stay: Call a bet.

Steal: A type of bluff usually made in late position.

Steaming: Playing badly as a result of an upset – see also On Tilt.

Straddle: An additional blind, the largest in the game. Often refers to a blind made voluntarily.

Straight: Five consecutive cards of different suits.

Straight Flush: Five consecutive cards of the same suit.

String Bet: An illegal bet in which a player puts some chips in the pot, then reaches back to his stack for more, without having first stated the full amount of his bet.

Strip Deck Poker: This is where certain cards are removed from the pack and play takes place without them. For instance, the 2s, 3s, 4s, 5s and 6s can be removed from the deck, making a 32-card deck. In the UK, five-card stud with a 32-card stripped deck was widely played until recently.

Suited: Cards of the same suit.

Super Satellite: A very small-stakes tournament where the winner(s) gains entry into a very big tournament. (See also Satellite.)

Sweeten the Pot: An archaic expression meaning to raise the pot (with a view to making it more attractive to win).

T

Table Stakes: A game of poker in which a player may use only the money on the table in front of him. This amount can be added to between, but not during, hands. Usually, players are not permitted to take money back off the table unless they are leaving the game.

Tap City: To be broke.

Tap Out: To bet all one's chips.

Tapped Out: To be broke.

Tell: A player's nervous mannerism or habitual behaviour which might give clues to his hand.

Texas Hold 'Em: A form of poker in which players use five community cards in combination with their two hole cards to form the best five-card hand. Also called Hold 'Em.

Third Pair: Pairing the third highest card on the flop/board. (Sometimes referred to as 'third button pair'.)

Three of a Kind: Three cards of the same rank, also called 'trips'.

Tight: A conservative player who only plays strong hands, or playing on fewer hands than the norm.

Tight Game: A game where there is a lot of conservative play, with small numbers of players in most pots.

Tilt: Going 'on tilt' means to loose control of one's emotions and play (uncharacteristically) badly. See also On Tilt.

Toke: An Americanism meaning a gratuity or tip.

Ton: £100.

Trey: A three of any suit.

Triplets: Three of a kind.

Trips: Slang for triplets; three of a kind.

Turn Card: The fourth communal card at Hold 'Em.

U

Under the Gun: The first player to act.

Under-Raise: To raise less than the previous bet, which is only allowed if a player is going all-in.

V

Value Bet: Betting with the hope that an opponent will call with a worse hand.

Vigarish: A charge made by a poker club for the facilities offered.

W

Wire: To inadvertently let someone know the value of your hand.

Wired Pair: A pair in the first two cards of any poker game.

Bibliography

The following books have helped the authors and are all recommended:

Alvarez, Al, *The Biggest Game in Town*, Fontana Paperbacks,1984.

Brunson, Doyle, et al., *Super System: A Course in Poker Power*, B & G Publishing, 1978.

Caro, Mike, *The Body Language of Poker*, (formerly called *Mike Caro's Book of Tells*), Gambling Times Inc., 1994.

Ciaffone, Bob, *Omaha Hold 'Em Poker (The Action Game)*, Self-published, 1992.

Fox, John, *Play Poker, Quit Work, and Sleep Till Noon*, Bacchus Press, California, USA, 1977.

Jessup, Richard, *The Cincinnati Kid*, Primus Donald I Fine, 1982.

McEvoy, Tom, *Tournament Poker*, Poker Plus Publications.

McNally, Brian, *Guidelines to the Universal Rules and Procedures of Poker*, Self-published, 1993.

May, Jesse, *Shut Up and Deal*, Anchor Books, 1998.

Malmuth, Mason, *Gambling Theory and Other Topics*, Two Plus Two Publishing, 1994.

Malmuth, Mason, *Poker Essays*, Two Plus Two Publishing, 1991.

Malmuth, Mason and Loomis, Lynne, *Fundamentals of Poker*, Two Plus Two Publishing, 1992.

Othmer, Konstantin, *The Elements of Seven-Card Stud*.

Reuben, Stewart and Ciaffone, Bob, *Pot-Limit and No-Limit Poker*, Self-published, 1997.

Sklansky, David, *Getting the Best of It*, Two Plus Two Publishing, 1989.

Sklansky, David, *Poker, Gaming, and Life*, Two Plus Two Publishing, 1997.

Sklansky, David, *The Theory of Poker*, (formerly called *Winning Poker*), Two Plus Two Publishing, 1992.

Sklansky, David and Malmuth, Mason, *Gambling for a Living*, Two Plus Two Publishing, 1997.

Sklansky, David, *Hold 'Em Poker*, Two Plus Two Publishing, 1996.

Sklansky, David, Malmuth, Mason and Zee, Ray, *Seven-Card Stud for Advanced Players*, Two Plus Two Publishing, 1994.

Spanier, David, *Total Poker*, Oldcastle Books, 1995.

Suzuki, Sylvester, *Poker Tournament Strategies*, Two Plus Two Publishing, 1998.

Yardley, Herbert O, *The Education of a Poker Player*, Orloff Press, 1997.

Zadeh, Norman, *Winning Poker Systems*, Wiltshire Book Company, 1977.

Zee, Ray, *High-Low-Split Poker, Seven-Card Stud and Omaha Eight-or Better, For Advanced Players*, Two Plus Two Publishing.